Document-Based Assessment for Global History

SECOND EDITION

Theresa C. Noonan

WALCH PUBLISHING

Acknowledgments

*The author wishes to thank all the publishers who granted permission
to use the quotations and illustrations that help bring history to life in this book.*

2   3   4   5   6   7   8   9   10

ISBN 978-0-8251-6337-1

Copyright © 1999, 2007

J. Weston Walch, Publisher

P.O. Box 658 • Portland, Maine 04104-0658

www.walch.com

Printed in the United States of America

CONTENTS

LETTER FROM THE AUTHOR

When I started the revisions for the original book, I wanted to include some of the changes that have been suggested by teachers. I also realized that the book lacked document-based questions on important topics in Asian history, as well as cross-topical questions. Since the original publication, I have learned much more about the importance of differentiating instruction so as to meet the needs of all the students in our classes. In addition, Advanced Placement World History has come online, and so I sought the advice of a friend and expert teacher of AP World History, Susan Daly. She made several suggestions which I feel make the book more useful to new AP World History teachers.

—Theresa C. Noonan

INTRODUCTION

Robin W. Winks, in *The Historian As Detective*, makes the analogy between the works of two professions—the historian and the detective. It is a link that we want students to make as we ask them to "do history." Just as historians become detectives as they work with clues from the past, students should learn to examine evidence, question its relevance, assess its validity, and then formulate hypotheses which they test further. Often these answers are challenged by others as they interpret the evidence and arrive at conflicting interpretations. Being a historical detective is challenging, engaging, and exciting work.

This book is designed to help teachers and students become better historians, thinkers, and writers. It provides them with opportunities to do the work of all three at one time. They examine evidence and data in order to arrive at informed and thoughtful positions, then present their thoughts clearly, logically, and effectively in writing. Although this is a challenging task, the required skills can be developed with practice—skills that we all need in order to be effective citizens and lifelong learners.

What Is a Document-Based Question, or DBQ?

A document-based question is a writing task in which a student analyzes significant evidence—documents and other data—to reach an informed position, then presents that information in a persuasive, logical, and accurate essay. The questions are generally open-ended, giving students the opportunity to develop responses to the questions using the documents and the information they have learned in their study of global history. The documents are mostly primary sources or eyewitness accounts provided by people who were actually "making history" or witnessing the events being examined. These primary sources include diaries, speeches, newspaper accounts, reports, and cartoons. Other documents considered primary sources are maps, photographs, graphs, and charts. In addition, secondary accounts or later interpretations of the events are included to provide different perspectives. Secondary accounts are written by people who have studied the primary

sources and reached conclusions based on the evidence. At times, these conclusions are contested by others who present conflicting interpretations, making for interesting analysis. Just as two eyewitnesses can disagree about what happened, historians also disagree and offer different interpretations about what happened and why it happened. Both primary sources and secondary accounts provide raw material for historians.

Why Use DBQs?

Document-based questions require students to think analytically when using the documents and to write responses that integrate information from a variety of sources. These are very important skills. Some of the skills involved in historical analysis include the following:

- evaluating the reliability, validity, and accuracy of historical sources

- identifying the point of view of these sources as well as determining bias

- identifying a problem or issue and considering alternative positions and solutions

- categorizing information as political, social, or economic, or as positive or negative

- comparing and contrasting different interpretations of key events

- constructing support for a position by choosing accurate, relevant evidence

Writing skills are crucial. Students need a process in place for addressing document-based questions. They need direct instruction using primary sources and conflicting interpretations of historical events, as well as repeated opportunities to practice these skills in class and in independent practice or homework. The students should be engaged in analyzing documents and writing in conjunction with documents almost daily.

The questions provided in this book can be used as a basis for class discussion or as preparation for a debate or seminar. They can be used for research projects or in extended writing tasks, as well as for

(continued)

formal assessment. These questions could also be used in the essay portion of a unit or final exam. If used as part of an assessment, it is important that students understand the expectations for this type of writing. Consequently, students must be familiar with the rubric that defines the criteria or characteristics of the content and skills required for each level of performance. A generic rubric has been included in this book (on pages *xi–xii*); however, it should be tailored to specific questions.

In addition, students benefit most if English and social studies teachers use a common vocabulary and integrate instruction to reinforce the appropriate thinking and writing skills in both classes. Students and teachers need to examine exemplary or "anchor" papers, and to reflect on their own development of writing skills. For that reason, student responses to several questions have been included in this book and can be used for instructional purposes. All students need to be effective thinkers and writers. Consequently, instructional strategies that develop these skills are important parts of every teacher's repertoire.

How to Use and Teach DBQs

The document-based questions in this book are suitable for use with high-school students and can be used in a variety of ways as described above. They may also be used with more able upper middle-school students who have been given enough practice with this format. Students usually have experience working with documents throughout their educational careers. Students in primary and intermediate grades work with age-appropriate artifacts, diaries, maps, and documents of all kinds. Consequently, when teachers at the middle- or high-school level engage students with these kinds of sources, they need to remind students that they have had plenty of experience in "doing history" with documents. The documents in this book may be complex or lengthy, but students can do this type of thinking and writing. Because of some students' lack of experience, teachers may want to further edit some of the documents or limit the number of documents they choose to use.

In the beginning, it is best to introduce the documents in this book as part of class instruction, so that the analytical skills can be taught directly or practiced in a supported environment. Each of the DBQs includes scaffolding in the form of questions that guide the student in interpreting the document and in addressing the main question or prompt. To help students develop these skills, teachers can use the documents as part of instruction on a particular topic. For example, the DBQ on ancient Greece, as well as pictures of representative art and architecture, can be used in daily lessons before it is used as a test question.

In addition to the documents with scaffolding, each DBQ is followed by a grading key. Several DBQs also include a ninth-grade student's work and teacher-assigned grades and comments. In addition, a Guide to Responding to Document-Based Questions has been included for students because it is important for them to have a process to use when addressing DBQs. With the guide, the rubric, the documents, the model student work, and the suggestions for instruction provided in this book, you are equipped to teach students how to write effective essays using documents.

Ideas for Lessons

At the beginning of the year, you many need to introduce or review the Guide for Responding to Document-Based Questions. At this time, it is important to use DBQs for instructional purposes so that students are comfortable and prepared to write DBQ essays when they are used as part of your assessment plan. Students should have the opportunity to review models of good essays. They should also be familiar with the rubric that you will be using to grade the essays.

In class lessons, use the documents as a basis for engaging the students in learning the essential information about a topic. You can add more visuals and artifacts to supplement those from this book in your daily lessons. For example, this process would work with DBQs dealing with the contributions of ancient Greece, the achievements of ancient Civilizations, Islamic civilization, and the civilizations of the Americas.

Use the documents as a basis for the instruction of an entire unit. For example, when teaching about the Industrial Revolution, have the students complete a graphic organizer of the essential-to-know concepts about the Industrial Revolution. Students begin by writing what they know or what questions they have about the topic before starting the unit. They will complete their graphic organizer

(continued)

after they have used the documents for each unit. For DBQ 12, for example, students might begin by asking themselves the following questions:

- What was the Industrial Revolution? Where did it begin, and why?

- What were the results of the Industrial Revolution (positive and negative)?

- How were the problems addressed or solved?

As another example, you could use a similar process to teach imperialism from different perspectives using DBQs 15, 16, and 17.

Set up learning stations by posting each document at a table or different place in the classroom and having students in small groups move from document to document. They will analyze the document together and respond to the scaffolding questions on their answer sheets before moving to the next document after a set time period.

Arrange the class in expert groups and assign each group a document to analyze and prepare to teach the rest of the class. This is a good way to help students prepare to write a response to an assigned DBQ.

Use a DBQ to review a topic across time and place. For example, to review human rights abuses, use DBQ 23. For global interaction, use DBQ 9.

Rewrite the task/question so it is more specific as to the number of examples students must include or the items they must address in their essay.

Use the DBQ as a basis for a seminar or debate. Rewrite the task so that it requires students to take a side or position. Specific DBQs that could be used in this way include the following:

- Imperialism in India: An Evaluation

- Imperialism in Africa: An Evaluation

- Causes of World War I

- Twentieth-Century China

Differentiating Instruction

The following ideas may help when working with students who are unfamiliar with DBQs, or who need extra support in working with documents.

Be sure that students understand the vocabulary by introducing new vocabulary before using the document. You may also need to provide a definition bank with each document.

Rewrite or adapt documents so that only the essential information is included.

Start by using two to four of the documents in a DBQ, and have students write a paragraph. Gradually add to the number of documents the students need to use. Have students practice writing a complete essay with introduction, body paragraph(s), and a conclusion. Start with two categories, and two documents for each category. Give students a graphic organizer or block to plan their response to the task.

Vary the test expectations or assignment. In lieu of having students write a complete essay, assign a mind map, outline, block, or other type of graphic organizer in which the student identifies the important information she or he will include from the documents and from outside information. Check the outline or graphic organizer for understanding and completeness. Another alternative to students writing a complete essay is for students to write the introductory paragraph and the first body paragraph after doing the organization or plan for writing.

To be sure that students are including information from the documents, teach them to cite the document they use. To ensure that students are including outside information, have them highlight it with a light-colored marker in the essay or paragraph.

(continued)

Document-Based Assessment for Global History

Ideas for the AP World History Teacher

Be aware that the DBQ for the AP World History exam has no scaffolding questions and that students are given approximately ten minutes to read and analyze five to six lengthy documents.

It is required that:

- Students write a clear, concise thesis statement in their introductory paragraph.

- Students use all documents and create two or three groups of documents.

- Students analyze and describe the point of view in two or three documents.

- Students create an additional document that is a missing point of view and explain why this document would help them write a better essay.

- Students put the essay topic into the larger picture of world history. Where does this selection of content fit within the larger picture of historical events across the world?

- Students finish the essay with a clear thesis restatement within their conclusion.

To adapt essays from this book for AP world history exam practice, you will need to reflect one of the particular themes that are identified for AP world history:

- Impact of interaction among major societies (trade, systems of international exchange, war and diplomacy)

- Impact of technology and demography on people and the environment (population growth and decline, disease, manufacturing, migration, agriculture, weaponry)

- The relationship of change and continuity across the world history period covered in the course, 8000 B.C.E. to the present

- Cultural and intellectual developments and interactions among and within societies

- Changes in functions and structures of states and attitudes toward states and political identities (political culture), including the emergence of the nation-state (types of political organizations)

Essays from this book can be adapted by adding documents or more evidence of point of view.

TO THE STUDENT

The document-based questions in this book are designed to help you become a skillful historian and a competent writer. You will examine real evidence about important questions in history. You will weigh this evidence against what you already know in order to reach a position. This process reflects what historians do. The skills you will practice are authentic to the analysis of history. You will examine primary source documents. You will analyze conflicting interpretations of historical events. You will interpret graphs, cartoons, maps, and charts. From all of this, you will then construct an understanding of an event or era. These are important skills for everyone to possess and to demonstrate.

Writing answers to DBQs will help you improve your complex reasoning skills. You will learn to detect bias, to weigh evidence, and to develop logical solutions. This process will guide you to express yourself in a clear, thoughtful, persuasive essay.

The Guide to Responding to Document-Based Questions included in this book provides you with a process to use whenever you are writing a DBQ essay. If you also want to know how your essay will be evaluated, the Scoring Rubric identifies the criteria used in grading your DBQ essay. Use this rubric to grade your essays before handing them in to your teacher. In addition, ask your teacher to duplicate a sample essay from this book or from your class so you can see a model essay.

You are now ready to begin. Start by reviewing the Guide to Responding to Document-Based Questions and the Scoring Rubric.

Guide to Responding to Document-Based Questions

A DBQ provides you with an opportunity to weigh significant evidence/documents to reach an informed position and to present the information in response to a question.

Process

1. Read the question carefully. What does the question ask you to do? Underline key words, eras, names, issues, or categories used in the question.

2. Write down the facts—names, dates, events—that you know about the topic and time period.

3. Read and analyze the documents. Write notes or respond to the scaffolding questions.

4. Reread the question, then consider the documents and your outside information.

5. Plan/organize your response using a block, outline, mind map, or other graphic organizer.

   - Identify the main subjects to be discussed in the body paragraphs.

   - Select the documents related to each topic.

   - Write down important information from the documents and from your outside knowledge of the topic.

(continued)

6. Write an organized essay responding to the question.

- Introductory paragraph: Take a stand on the question. Respond to all parts of the question. Develop your thesis. To what degree is it true? Provide background and explanation and definition of terms used in the question. Introduce the topics you will discuss in the body of your essay.

- Body paragraphs: Use a separate paragraph for each topic, issue, or argument. Include specific examples to support generalizations or to make distinctions. Cite specific evidence from the documents, but avoid long quotations. Integrate information from the documents and from your knowledge in responding to the questions.

- Concluding paragraph: Restate your position and main ideas that you presented in your essay.

GENERIC SCORING RUBRIC

5	• Thoroughly develops all aspects of the task evenly and in depth • Is more analytical than descriptive (analyzes, evaluates, and/or creates information) • Incorporates relevant information from at least ___ documents • Incorporates substantial relevant outside information • Richly supports the theme with many relevant facts, examples, and details • Demonstrates a logical and clear plan of organization; includes an introduction and a conclusion that go beyond a restatement of the theme
4	• Develops all aspects of the task but may do so somewhat unevenly • Is both descriptive and analytical • Incorporates relevant information from at least ___ documents • Incorporates relevant outside information • Supports the theme with relevant facts, examples, and details • Demonstrates a logical and clear plan of organization; includes an introduction and a conclusion that go beyond a restatement of the theme
3	• Develops all aspects of the task with little depth or develops most aspects • Is both descriptive and analytical (applies, analyzes, evaluates, and/or creates information) • Incorporates relevant information from at least ___ documents • Incorporates relevant outside information • Includes some relevant facts, examples, and details; may include some minor inaccuracies • Demonstrates a satisfactory plan of organization; includes an introduction and a conclusion that may be a restatement of the theme
2	• Minimally develops all aspects of the task or develops some aspects of the task in some depth • Is primarily descriptive; may include faulty, weak, or isolated application or analysis • Incorporates limited relevant information from the documents or consists primarily or relevant information copied from the documents • Presents little or no relevant outside information • Includes few relevant facts, examples, and details; may include some inaccuracies • Demonstrates a general plan of organization; may lack focus; may contain digressions; may not clearly identify which aspect of the task is being addressed; may lack an introduction and/or a conclusion

(continued)

1	• Minimally develops some aspects of the task • Is descriptive; may lack understanding, application, or analysis • Makes vague, unclear references to the documents or consists primarily of relevant and irrelevant information copied from the documents • Shows limited understanding of the task with vague, unclear references to the documents • Presents no relevant outside information • Includes few relevant facts, examples, or details; may include inaccuracies • May demonstrate a weakness in organization; may lack focus; may contain digressions; may not clearly identify which aspect of the task is being addressed; may lack an introduction and/or a conclusion
0	• Fails to develop the task or may only refer to the theme in a general way; OR includes no relevant facts, examples, or details; OR includes only the historical context and/or task as copied from the book; OR includes only entire documents copied from the book; OR is illegible; OR is a blank paper

* Provided by the New York State Education Department (revised, 2004)

DBQ 1: ACHIEVEMENTS OF ANCIENT CIVILIZATIONS

Historical Context

Early civilizations arose in the river valleys of Mesopotamia, Egypt, China, and India. These earliest civilizations made important and lasting contributions to humankind.

■ **Directions:** The following question is based on the accompanying documents in Part A. As you analyze each document, take into account both the source of the document and the author's point of view. Be sure to do each of the following steps:

1. Carefully read the document-based question. Consider what you already know about this topic. How would you answer the question if you had no documents to examine?

2. Read each document carefully, underlining key phrases and words that address the document-based question. You may also wish to use the margin to make brief notes. Answer the questions that follow each document before moving on to the next document.

3. Based on your own knowledge and on the information in the documents, formulate a thesis that directly answers the question.

4. Organize supportive and relevant information into a brief outline.

5. Write a well-organized essay proving your thesis. You should present your essay logically. Include information both from the documents and from your own knowledge beyond the documents.

Question: Choose three ancient civilizations. What were the achievements of each of these civilizations? How did each of these civilizations make lasting contributions to humankind?

 PART A The following documents provide information about the achievements of several ancient civilizations. Examine each document carefully. In the space provided, answer the question or questions that follow each document.

DBQ 1: ACHIEVEMENTS OF ANCIENT CIVILIZATIONS

Document 1

This document describes the accomplishments of the Sumerians.

> The Sumerians lived in southern Mesopotamia. They built a number of cities. Because they lacked stone and timber, they used mud bricks to build walled cities, temples, and palaces. Their architectural innovations included arches, columns, ramps, and the pyramid-shaped ziggurat. These new features and styles influenced building throughout Mesopotamia. In addition, the Sumerians developed copper and bronze tools and weapons. They also developed the world's first known writing, cuneiform. They used it on clay tablets.

Source: Bech, Black, Krieger, Naylor, Shabaka, *World History: Patterns of Interaction,* McDougal Littell, 1999 (adapted)

What were three accomplishments of the Sumerians?

_____

_____

_____

_____

What impact did Sumerian accomplishments have on other civilizations?

_____

_____

_____

_____

(continued)

DBQ 1: ACHIEVEMENTS OF ANCIENT CIVILIZATIONS

Document 2

This document provides information about the Code of Hammurabi.

> Hammurabi was the king of Babylon in Mesopotamia. He set up one of the earliest written sets of laws in history. It is called the Code of Hammurabi. It covered almost everything that affected the community, including family relations, business conduct, and crime. Hammurabi wanted to unify his empire and provide order and protection for the weak. This provided a model for other far-flung empires. Some of the laws were:
>
> • If a man destroys the eye of another man, they shall destroy his eye.
>
> • If a son strikes his father, they shall cut off his hand.
>
> • If two people have a disagreement, both will go before a judge for a decision. If one of these people does not like the judge's ruling, then he has the right to appeal to a higher court.

Source: Bech, Black, Krieger, Naylor, Shabaka, *World History: Patterns of Interaction*, McDougal Littell, 1999 (adapted)

What type of legal system did Hammurabi set up?

_____

_____

_____

_____

Why did Hammurabi want to set up a system of laws?

_____

_____

_____

What impact did the Code of Hammurabi have on world cultures?

_____

_____

_____

_____

(continued)

DBQ 1: ACHIEVEMENTS OF ANCIENT CIVILIZATIONS

Document 3

The excerpt below describes farming in ancient Egypt.

> Farmers in ancient Egypt developed a system of watering their fields using the water from the Nile River. They built dams and dug ditches or canals to move the water into their fields. The farmers also built reservoirs in which they collected water. They raised water from the pools into the irrigation ditches with a shaduf, a weighted pole with a bucket on one end. The bucket was filled with water and then swung around and emptied into the irrigation ditch. This technology continues to be used in many parts of the Middle East to increase the amount of arable land.

According to the excerpt, what technology is being used?

_____

_____

_____

_____

How does this technology work?

_____

_____

_____

_____

How did this technology contribute to later societies?

_____

_____

_____

_____

(continued)

DBQ 1: ACHIEVEMENTS OF ANCIENT CIVILIZATIONS

Document 4

This document provides information about Egyptian pyramids.

> Pyramids were built as a final resting place for the *ka,* or spirit, of the pharaoh. The embalmed body of the pharaoh was placed in a special room within the pyramid. Also in the room were gold, jewels, chariots, statues, and other objects the pharaoh might need in the afterlife. Pyramids were built of huge blocks of stone that were moved into place by groups of peasants and other workers. The government organized and directed these armies of workers.

Source: Bech, Black, Krieger, Naylor, Shabaka, *World History: Patterns of Interaction,* McDougal Littell, 1999 (adapted)

Why were the pyramids built?

_____

_____

_____

How were the pyramids built?

_____

_____

_____

Document 5

This document provides information about the Chinese writing system.

> Chinese, like other early writing systems developed from pictographs, simplified drawings of objects. Other characters were developed to stand for ideas and parts of words. The writing system used in China today is directly related to this earlier pictographic writing. China was a very large and diverse area. Having a common written language made it possible to unify these lands and peoples.

Source: Bech, Black, Krieger, Naylor, Shabaka, *World History: Patterns of Interaction,* McDougal Littell, 1999 (adapted)

(continued)

DBQ 1: ACHIEVEMENTS OF ANCIENT CIVILIZATIONS

How would you describe the Chinese system of writing?

_____

_____

What impact did a written language have on China?

_____

_____

Document 6

This document provides information about planned cities on the Indus River.

> Archaeologists have found ruins of many cities along the Indus River. They
> date these cities back to about 2000 B.C.E. The largest cities were Mohenjo-
> Daro and Harappa. These cities were laid out along a precise grid with a
> fortified citadel and a separate section for residential housing. Engineers
> provided indoor plumbing and sewer systems so that most houses had
> private bathrooms and toilets.

Source: Bech, Black, Krieger, Naylor, Shabaka, *World History: Patterns of Interaction,*
McDougal Littell, 1999 (adapted)

What made the cities along the Indus unusual for their time?

_____

_____

What impact did this urban planning have on later civilizations?

_____

_____

PART B Choose three ancient civilizations. What were the achievements of each of
these civilizations? How did each of these civilizations make lasting
contributions to humankind?

DBQ 1: TEACHER PAGE

Grading Key

Document 1

Accomplishments of the Sumerians (students name three): built cities, temples, palaces; developed architectural innovations such as arches, columns, ramps, and ziggurats; developed copper and bronze weapons; developed the world's first known writing—cuneiform. Other civilizations used the architectural innovations in their buildings, adapted cuneiform to create writing systems for their own languages, and spread Sumerian literature and learning across the Middle East. They may also have acquired knowledge of working with copper and bronze from the Sumerians.

Document 2

Hammurabi set up a uniform legal system that covered almost everything that affected the community. It covered business disputes, family relations, crime, and other issues. Although it was in some ways harsh, everyone knew the consequences of their actions. Hammurabi wanted to unify his empire with one legal system. He wanted to protect the people and provide order. Other cultures that wanted to unify their people adopted a single legal system.

Document 3

This excerpt describes farmers using a shadouf to irrigate their fields. They have built irrigation canals to bring water to all fields. The shadouf lifts the water out and dumps it into the irrigation canals. The technology was used by farmers in other societies to water their fields.

Document 4

The pyramids were built as a resting place after death for the *ka*, or spirit, of the pharaoh. The embalmed body of the pharaoh was buried in a special room within the pyramid along with jewels, gold, and other objects needed for the afterlife. The government organized peasants into groups who built the huge monuments by moving the stone blocks into place.

Document 5

The Chinese writing system is pictographic, which means it is based on simple drawings of the object. The writing system used today is similar to the ancient one. Having a common writing system made it easier to unify China.

(continued)

Document 6

The cities along the Indus were unusual because they were planned and laid out in a grid. Also, the cities included indoor plumbing and sewer systems. Later civilizations often built cities around a fortified citadel. Also in the modern era (nineteenth and twentieth centuries), cities were built with plumbing and sewer systems provided by the government.

Additional Information Beyond the Documents

These documents provide students with only fragments of evidence. Essays should include relevant information beyond the documents—information that students have learned from their classroom study, outside reading and viewing, and other learning experiences. The following table suggests some of that information.

Mesopotamia (Sumerian and Babylonian)	Egypt	China	Indus
• buildings • tools • belief systems • governmental systems • irrigation • systems science • technology	• governmental system • irrigation • religious beliefs • writing • science • technology • pyramids • architectural design	• writing system • bronze and iron tools • weapons and religious utensils • silk and rice production • governmental system	• governmental system • engineering • architecture

DBQ 2: ANCIENT GREEK CONTRIBUTIONS

Historical Context

Many of the roots of Western civilization can be traced back to the ancient Greeks. They made long-lasting contributions in the areas of art, architecture, philosophy, math, drama, and science.

■ **Directions:** The following question is based on the accompanying documents in Part A. As you analyze the documents, take into account both the source of each document and the author's point of view. Be sure to do each of the following steps:

1. Carefully read the document-based question. Consider what you already know about this topic. How would you answer the question if you had no documents to examine?

2. Read each document carefully, underlining key phrases and words that address the document-based question. You may also wish to use the margin to make brief notes. Answer the questions that follow each document before moving on to the next document.

3. Based on your own knowledge and on the information in the documents, formulate a thesis that directly answers the document-based question.

4. Organize supportive and relevant information into a brief outline.

5. Write a well-organized essay proving your thesis. You should present your essay logically. Include information both from the documents and from your own knowledge beyond the documents.

Question: What did the ancient Greeks contribute to Western civilization?

PART A

The following documents will help you understand the contributions of the ancient Greeks. Examine each document carefully. In the space provided, answer the question or questions that follow each document.

(continued)

DBQ 2: ANCIENT GREEK CONTRIBUTIONS

Document 1

This adapted quotation is from Socrates, who lived from about 470 to about 399 B.C.E.

> The unexamined life is not worth living.

Who was Socrates, and what was he suggesting in this quote?

_____

_____

_____

_____

Document 2

This adapted quotation is from Aristotle, who lived in Greece from 384 to 322 B.C.E.

> Since human reason is the most godlike part of human nature, a life guided
> by human reason is superior to any other. . . . For man, this is the life of
> reason, since the faculty of reason is the distinguishing characteristic of
> human beings.

Who was Aristotle, and what did he believe about human nature?

_____

_____

_____

_____

(continued)

DBQ 2: ANCIENT GREEK CONTRIBUTIONS

Document 3

This adapted excerpt is from Pericles' funeral oration, given to the people of Athens in about 430 B.C.E.

> Our plan of government favors the many instead of the few: that is why it is called a democracy. . . .
>
> As for social standing, advancement is open to everyone, according to ability. While every citizen has an equal opportunity to serve the public, we reward our most distinguished citizens by asking them to make our political decisions. Nor do we discriminate against the poor. A man may serve his country no matter how low his position on the social scale.

What type of government was Pericles describing? What were his expectations for citizens in this type of government?

_____

_____

_____

_____

Document 4

The following is an adapted excerpt from The Hippocratic Oath. Hippocrates, who created this oath, lived from about 460 to about 377 B.C.E.

> I will follow that [treatment] which, according to my ability and judgment, I will consider for the benefit of my patients, and abstain from whatever is [harmful].
>
> I will give no deadly medicine to anyone if asked, nor suggest any such [advice]. . . .

Who was Hippocrates, and what was he promising to do?

_____

_____

_____

_____

(continued)

DBQ 2: ANCIENT GREEK CONTRIBUTIONS

Document 5

This excerpt is adapted from the *Elements,* written by Euclid in about 300 B.C.E.

> Proposition 15, THEOREM: If two straight lines cut one another, the vertical, or opposite, angles shall be equal.

Who was Euclid, and what has been the impact of his work?

_____

_____

_____

_____

Document 6

This excerpt is adapted from the play *Antigone* by Sophocles, written in about 441 B.C.E. In this play, Antigone defies the king's order and buries her brother, who was killed while leading a rebellion.

> Creon: And still you dared to overstep these laws?
>
> Antigone: For me, it was not Zeus who made that order. Nor do I think your orders were so strong that you, a mortal man, could overrun the gods' unwritten and unfailing laws. . . . I know I must die . . . but if I left my brother dead and unburied, I'd have cause to grieve as now I grieve not.

What values are expressed in this Greek play?

_____

_____

_____

_____

(continued)

12

DBQ 2: ANCIENT GREEK CONTRIBUTIONS

Document 7

Examine this photograph of a famous Greek building, the Parthenon.

How have specific features of this building influenced Western civilization?

_____

_____

_____

_____

(continued)

DBQ 2: ANCIENT GREEK CONTRIBUTIONS

Document 8

Myron's famous marble sculpture, *Discus Thrower (Discobolus)*, represents an Olympic event. Myron created this sculpture around 460–450 B.C.E.

What does this statue reveal about Greek values?

_____

_____

_____

_____

PART B   What did the ancient Greeks contribute to Western civilization?

DBQ 2: TEACHER PAGE

Grading Key

Document 1

Socrates was a philosopher from Athens. He believed that a person must ask questions and seek to understand life.

Document 2

Aristotle was also a philosopher. He believed that reason is what makes human beings "superior" to other living things. Reason makes human beings unique.

Document 3

Pericles was describing a democracy where everyone (in the case of ancient Greece, this meant just nonslave men) had an equal opportunity to advance and to serve their country. However, everyone was also expected to participate in civic affairs regardless of their social position.

Document 4

Hippocrates was a Greek doctor who promised that he would provide only medical care that helped his patients. This expresses the responsibility placed on doctors that continues today.

Document 5

Euclid was a Greek mathematician. His ideas were the basis for the field of geometry, which is studied around the world today.

Document 6

This drama shows the important role that the gods played in Greek life. Antigone felt she had to obey her conscience rather than the laws of mortal men.

Document 7

The Parthenon has the columns and pediment that characterize Greek architecture. The balance and simplicity of lines are now evident in government buildings around the world, particularly in the West.

(continued)

DBQ 2: TEACHER PAGE

Document 8

This marble statue of the Discobolus is evidence of the Greek interest in a perfect human body. It also shows the Greek interest in physical activities and skills, which were demonstrated in Olympic competition.

Additional Information Beyond the Documents

These documents provide students with only fragments of evidence. Essays should include relevant information beyond the documents—information that students have learned from their classroom study, outside reading and viewing, and other supplemental activities. The following table suggests some of the concepts, people, and events from students' outside learning that they might include in their essays.

Students may include their own knowledge of individuals such as Plato, Aristotle, and Homer, and contributions in the areas of drama, poetry, historical writing, architecture, sculpture, philosophy, mathematics, and science.

Architecture • Parthenon • Acropolis	**Mythology**
Democracy • Athens (Pericles)	**Olympic Games**
Drama—Tragedies • Sophocles • Euripides • Aeschylus	**Philosophy** • Socrates • Plato • Aristotle
Math and Science • Euclid • Pythagoras • Archimedes • Hippocrates	

DBQ 3: FALL OF THE WESTERN ROMAN EMPIRE

Historical Context

In the third century C.E., Rome faced many problems. In addition to internal decay, the invasion by Germanic tribes seemed to sound the death knell for the Western Roman Empire. Historians have examined both the internal conditions that weakened the expansive empire and the external force of the barbarian invasions. From this, historians have developed a variety of explanations for the fall of the Western Roman Empire.

■ **Directions:** The following question is based on the accompanying documents in Part A. As you analyze the documents, take into account both the source of each document and the author's point of view. Be sure to do each of the following steps:

1. Carefully read the document-based question. Consider what you already know about this topic. How would you answer the question if you had no documents to examine?

2. Read each document carefully, underlining key phrases and words that address the document-based question. You may also wish to use the margin to make brief notes. Answer the questions that follow each document before moving on to the next document.

3. Based on your own knowledge and on the information in the documents, formulate a thesis that directly answers the document-based question.

4. Organize supportive and relevant information into a brief outline.

5. Write a well-organized essay proving your thesis. You should present your essay logically. Include information both from the documents and from your own knowledge beyond the documents.

Question: What caused the fall of the Western Roman Empire?

PART A   The following documents address the causes for the fall of Rome. Examine each document carefully. In the space provided, answer the question or questions that follow each document.

(continued)

DBQ 3: FALL OF THE WESTERN ROMAN EMPIRE

Document 1

This adapted excerpt describes the Western Roman Empire.

> The basic trouble was that very few inhabitants of the empire believed that the old civilization was worth saving . . . . [T]he overwhelming majority of the population had been systematically excluded from political responsibilities. They could not organize to protect themselves; they could not serve in the army. . . . Their economic plight was hopeless. Most of them were serfs bound to the soil, and the small urban groups saw their cities slipping into uninterrupted decline

Source: Strayer, Gatzke, and Harbison, *The Course of Civilization*, Harcourt, Brace and World, Inc., 1961 (adapted)

What were the basic problems facing the Western Roman Empire, according to these authors?

_____

_____

_____

Document 2

This adapted excerpt describes the fall of the Roman Empire.

> The decline of Rome was the natural and inevitable effect of immoderate greatness [large size]. . . . The introduction . . . of Christianity had some influence on the decline and fall of the Roman empire. The clergy successfully preached the doctrine of patience; the active virtues of society were discouraged; and the last remains of military spirit were buried in the cloister; a large portion of public and private wealth was consecrated to the . . . demands of charity and devotion. . . .

Source: Edward Gibbon, *The Decline and Fall of the Roman Empire*, 1776–88 (adapted)

According to this excerpt from Gibbon, what were two causes for the fall of Rome? Explain both.

_____

_____

_____

(continued)

DBQ 3: FALL OF THE WESTERN ROMAN EMPIRE

Document 3

This excerpt described economic factors in the Roman Empire.

> First the economic factor . . . While the empire was expanding, its prosperity was fed by plundered wealth and by new markets in the semi-barbaric provinces. When the empire ceased to expand, however, economic progress soon ceased. . . .
>
> The abundance of slaves led to the growth of the latifundia, the great estates that . .,. came to dominate agriculture and ruin the free coloni [farmers], who drifted to the cities, to add to the unemployment there. The abundance of slaves likewise kept wages low.

Source: Herbert J. Muller, *Uses of the Past*, Signet, 1967 (adapted)

What economic issues did Muller identify as causes for decline? Explain.

_____

_____

_____

In what ways was slavery a cause for the decline of the Roman Empire?

_____

_____

Document 4

This excerpt blames the decline of the Roman Empire on the heavy taxation required to support the government's expenses.

> Part of the money went into . . . the maintenance of the army and of the vast bureaucracy required by a centralized government. . . . [T]he expense led to strangling taxation. . . . The heart was taken out of enterprising men . . . tenants fled from their farms and businessmen and workmen from their occupations. Private enterprise was crushed and the state was forced to take over many kinds of business to keep the machine running. People learned to expect something for nothing. The old Roman virtues of self-reliance and initiative were lost in that part of the population on relief [welfare]. . . . The central government undertook such far-reaching responsibility in affairs that the fiber of the citizens weakened.

Source: Henry Haskell, *The New Deal in Old Rome*, A.A. Knopf, 1947 (adapted)

(continued)

DBQ 3: FALL OF THE WESTERN ROMAN EMPIRE

Why did the Roman government have large expenses?

_____

_____

What was the effect of high taxation on the people?

_____

_____

What effect did the establishment of a governmental welfare system have on the people?

_____

_____

Document 5

This excerpt blames the fall on "internal decay," specifically that of the military.

> Rome, like all great empires, was not overthrown by external enemies but undermined by internal decay. . . . The military crisis was the result of . . . proud old aristocracy's . . . shortage of children. [Consequently,] foreigners poured into this . . . void [lack of soldiers]. The Roman army [was] composed entirely of Germans.

Source: Indro Montanelli, *Romans Without Laurels,* Pantheon Books, 1962 (adapted)

What did this author identify as the cause of problems in the military?

_____

_____

_____

(continued)

DBQ 3: FALL OF THE WESTERN ROMAN EMPIRE

Document 6

This map shows the barbarian invasions of the Roman Empire prior to 476.

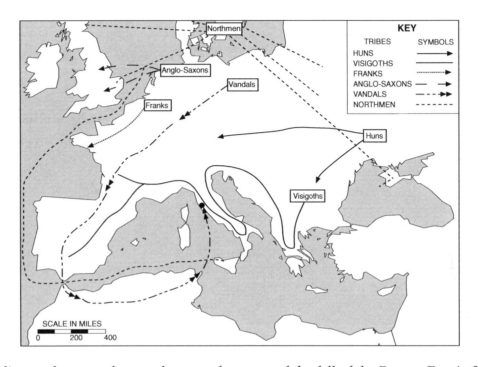

According to the map above, what was the cause of the fall of the Roman Empire?

_____

_____

_____

Was this a unified attack? Explain.

_____

_____

_____

PART B

What caused the fall of the Western Roman Empire?

Grading Key

Document 1

The Romans did not feel the empire was worth saving. They became apathetic. The majority were serfs and had been excluded from the government and from the army. Farming was declining, and so were the cities.

Document 2

The Roman Empire fell because it was too large in size. It had conquered too much territory and was unable to keep control over the many parts. In addition, Christianity weakened the empire because it required its followers to be spiritual and peaceful, not active in civic affairs or the military. It also encouraged both people and the government to spend for religious rather than civic purposes.

Document 3

When the empire stopped expanding, its markets also stopped expanding, and no new plundered wealth entered the empire. Economic progress ended. Slave labor allowed huge estates to take the place of small farms. Small farmers became either tenant farmers or unemployed city dwellers.

Document 4

The government needed money for the army, the huge bureaucracy, and welfare. High taxation drove private owners out of business. The government was forced to take over many of these businesses. People on welfare lost their initiative, and this weakened the moral fiber of the empire.

Document 5

The problem in the military was the shortage of Roman citizens available to be soldiers, because of a low birth rate among the aristocracy, and the resulting inclusion of Germans in their places.

Document 6

The map shows the barbarian invasions of the Roman Empire, which was an important factor in the fall of the empire. It was not a unified attack—the map shows that the barbarians attacked the empire on all sides.

(continued)

DBQ 3: TEACHER PAGE

Additional Information Beyond the Documents

These documents provide students with only fragments of evidence. Essays should include relevant information from beyond the documents—information that students have learned from their classroom study. The following table suggests some of the concepts, people, and events from students' outside learning that they might include in their essays.

Overall	Political	Social	Economic
• The multiple causes and conditions in the Western Roman Empire—political, social, economic, and military—that led to the fall • The Germanic tribes • The gradual decline, rather than "fall," of the Western Roman Empire	• Lack of orderly succession for emperors • Government corruption • Extensive empire difficult to rule/run	• Lack of patriotism, morality • Luxury of wealthy • Class distinctions	• Small farmers losing their land • Increases in welfare for unemployed • Heavy taxation • Increases in slavery

Sample Student Essay

Although the Roman Empire was truly affected by external threats, I believe that it fell as a result of internal decay. Two influential internal causes of the fall were economy and social issues. Slavery, high taxes, and government spending contributed to economic decline. Also the attitudes of the people greatly affected the future of the already weakening Western Roman Empire.

First, the economy proved to be a factor in the decline of the empire. Slavery was the cause of a great increase in unemployment, as the use of slaves in the workforce took over the jobs of peasants and "ruined the free peasantry" (*Document 3*). Many people lost their businesses and jobs (*Document 3*). Another economic situation involved the government and its high taxes, as well as spending. The central government of the Roman Empire was forced to increase taxes, as the price of keeping up the large empire increased. "There were land taxes, property taxes,

(continued)

occupation taxes, poll taxes" (*Document 4*). The high taxes were difficult to manage, and again, many were left poor. However, government spending was also a problem. Money the government earned from taxes went mainly to the "bureaucracy required by a central government," and the ". . . maintenance of the army" (*Document 4*). In addition, social situations also contributed to the fall of the Roman Empire.

Social issues, including the spread of Christianity as well as the feelings of the people toward the Roman Empire, greatly influenced the decline. As Christianity spread throughout the empire, the outlook of people on life and the treatment of others changed. "Love thy neighbor" and salvation in order to reach heaven caused the people to become more thoughtful of others and less devoted to the emperor. This situation hurt the military, where "remains of military spirit were buried in the cloister" (*Document 2*). These men lost their fight, their war-like ways as this new religion taught the evilness and sin in hurting others. Thus, the military grew weak. Also, the people of the empire had a poor outlook concerning the future on earth. As a result of the internal decay that was obvious in the major cities of the empires, ". . . very few inhabitants of the empire believed that the old civilization was worth saving" (*Document 1*). When the people living in the empire could not find pride for their land, the empire began to weaken, as people either left or did not get involved in the central government's efforts to try to improve certain situations.

In conclusion, the combined economic and social conflict truly influenced the fall of the Western Roman Empire. I firmly believe that issues such as slavery, taxes, and the spread of Christianity caused defeat for this once strong and powerful empire. It has been said that Rome wasn't built in a day, but also true was that it didn't fall in one day either. This process of decay and corruption occurred over a period of 100 years. But still, the strongest empire in the world fell, never to be repeated again.

Teacher Comments

This essay addresses the required aspects of the topic—internal or external causes for the fall of the Western Roman Empire. It includes relevant outside details, facts, and examples. The writer incorporates the outside information and the documents into the body of a well-organized essay, which includes an introduction and conclusion.

Score: 5

This is a good DBQ essay written early in the ninth grade as part of a unit test.

Name _____   Date _____

DBQ 4: THE MIDDLE AGES: DARK AGES, AGE OF FAITH, AGE OF FEUDALISM, OR A GOLDEN AGE?

Historical Context

The Middle Ages in Europe, a period of time from approximately 500 to 1400 B.C.E., have been referred to by a variety of terms—the Age of Faith, the Dark Ages, the Age of Feudalism, and even a Golden Age. The medieval era began with the destruction of the Roman Empire and the disorder that followed, which led to the rise of feudalism. During this period of darkness, the Roman Catholic Church provided spiritual direction as well as many nonreligious functions for the people of the times. Many literary, artistic, and architectural advances occurred.

■ **Directions:** The following question is based on the accompanying documents in Part A. As you analyze the documents, take into account both the source of each document and the author's point of view. Be sure to do each of the following steps:

1. Carefully read the document-based question. Consider what you already know about this topic. How would you answer the question if you had no documents to examine?

2. Read each document carefully, underlining key phrases and words that address the document-based question. You may also wish to use the margin to make brief notes. Answer the questions which follow each document.

3. Based on your own knowledge and on the information found in the documents, formulate a thesis that directly answers the question.

4. Organize supportive and relevant information into a brief outline.

5. Write a well-organized essay proving your thesis. The essay should be logically presented and should include information both from the documents and from your own knowledge outside of the documents.

> **Question: Which labels for the Middle Ages best describe the era between 500 and 1400 in Europe: The Dark Ages, the Age of Feudalism, the Age of Faith, or the Golden Age of Europe? You must discuss three labels.**

 PART A The following documents provide information about the Middle Ages in Europe. Examine each document carefully, and answer the questions that follow.

(continued)

DBQ 4: THE MIDDLE AGES: DARK AGES, AGE OF FAITH, AGE OF FEUDALISM, OR A GOLDEN AGE?

Document 1

This excerpt describes Europe in the ninth and tenth centuries.

> The barbarians have broken through the ramparts. The Saracen [Moors] invasions have spread in successive waves over the South. The Hungarians swarm over the Eastern provinces . . . they sacked town and village, and laid waste the fields. They burned down the churches and then departed with a crowd of captives. . . . There is no longer any trade, only unceasing terror. . . . The peasant has abandoned his ravaged fields to avoid the violence of anarchy. The people have gone to cower in the depths of the forests or in inaccessible regions, or have taken refuge in the high mountains. . . . Society has no longer any government. . . .

Source: *The Middle Ages*, Frantz Funck-Brentano, Heinemann, 1922 (adapted)

According to the author, what were conditions like in Europe during the 800s?

_____

_____

_____

Document 2

This excerpt is from the Homage Oath taken by John of Toul.

> I, John of Toul, make known that I am the liege man of the [count and countess of Champagne]. . . . I will aid the count of Champagne in my own person, and will send to the count and countess of Champagne the knights whose service I owe to them for the fief which I hold of them. . . ."

Source: Fealty by John of Toul to Theobald, Count of Champagne, thirteenth century (adapted)

What are the obligations John is promising to uphold?

_____

_____

(continued)

DBQ 4: THE MIDDLE AGES: DARK AGES, AGE OF FAITH, AGE OF FEUDALISM, OR A GOLDEN AGE?

Document 3

The ninth-century *Anglo-Saxon Chronicle* tells of invasions of England.

> 842   In this year there was a great slaughter in London and Quentavic and in Rochester.
>
> 846   According to their custom the Northmen plundered . . . and burned the town of Dordrecht. . . . the Northmen, with their boats filled with immense booty, including both men and goods, returned to their own country. . . .

According to this Chronicle, what is happening at this time (842–846)?

_____

_____

_____

Document 4

Feudal Obligations

Vassel to Lord		Lord to Vassel
• Loyalty	⟶	• Protection
• Military Service	⟵	• Land (fief)
• Ransom, if needed		

Explain the mutual obligation(s) as illustrated in this diagram.

_____

_____

_____

(continued)

DBQ 4: THE MIDDLE AGES: DARK AGES, AGE OF FAITH, AGE OF FEUDALISM, OR A GOLDEN AGE?

Document 5

A Church council calls for the observance of the Truce of God, 1083.

> That from the first day of the Advent of our Lord through Epiphany . . . and throughout the year on every Sunday, Friday, and Saturday, and on the fast days of the four seasons . . . this decree of peace shall be observed . . . so that no one may commit murder, arson, robbery, or assault, no one may injure another with a sword, club, or any kind of weapon. . . . On . . . every day set aside, or to be set aside, for fasts or feasts, arms may be carried, but on this condition, that no injury shall be done in any way to any one . . . If it shall happen that any castle is besieged during the days which are included within the peace, the besiegers shall cease from attack unless they are set upon by the beseiged and compelled to beat the latter back. . . .

According to this document, what is the Church trying to accomplish?

_____

_____

_____

Document 6

This excerpt describes the Middle Ages.

> . . . we learn that an age once traditionally described as "dark" had remarkable vitality and exuberance. Even at its worst it performed the function of guarding, frequently by accident and chance, the knowledge and treasures of what had come before, but even more it was creative and inventive, and transmitted to later ages great riches of its own.

Source: Gray C. Boyce, *The 34th Yearbook of the National Council for the Social Studies,* "The Medieval Period," 1964 (adapted)

What functions were provided during the Middle Ages according to this author?

_____

_____

_____

(continued)

DBQ 4: THE MIDDLE AGES: DARK AGES, AGE OF FAITH, AGE OF FEUDALISM, OR A GOLDEN AGE?

Document 7

This excerpt describes some of the positive aspects of the Middle Ages.

> . . . Medieval culture was imperfect, was restricted to a narrow circle of superior minds. . . . Measure it, however, by the memories and the achievements that it has bequeathed to the modern world, and it will be found not unworthy to rank with those of earlier and later Golden Ages. It flourished in the midst of rude surroundings, fierce passions, and material ambitions . . . we must judge of them by their philosophy and law, by their poetry and architecture. . . .

Source: H.C. Davis, *Medieval Europe*, Oxford University Press, 1946 (adapted)

How does this author describe the era?

_____

_____

_____

Document 8

This excerpt is adapted from the fourteenth-century monastic vows of Brother Gerard.

> I hereby renounce my parents, my brothers and relatives, my friends, my possessions . . . and the vain and empty glory and pleasure of this world. I also renounce my own will, for the will of God. I accept all the hardships of the monastic life, and take the vows of purity, chastity, and poverty, in the hope of heaven; and I promise to remain a monk in this monastery all the days of my life.

What is Gerald promising to do when he becomes a monk?

_____

_____

_____

(continued)

DBQ 4: THE MIDDLE AGES: DARK AGES, AGE OF FAITH, AGE OF FEUDALISM, OR A GOLDEN AGE?

Document 9

In 1095, Pope Urban II issued a call for a holy crusade—a war to recapture the Holy Land.

> Your brethren who live in the [Middle] East are in urgent need of your help. . . . For, as most of you have heard, the Turks and the Arabs have attacked them and have conquered the territory of Romania [the Byzantine Empire]. . . . They have occupied more and more of the lands of those Christians. . . . They have killed and captured many, and have destroyed the churches and devastated the Empire. . . . All who die by the way, whether by land or sea, or in battle against the pagans, shall have immediate remission of sins.

Source: Pope Urban II to the Council of Clermont, 1095 (adapted)

How does this call for a crusade demonstrate the power of the Pope and the Catholic Church?

_____

_____

_____

_____

_____

(continued)

DBQ 4: THE MIDDLE AGES: DARK AGES, AGE OF FAITH, AGE OF FEUDALISM, OR A GOLDEN AGE?

Document 10

Examine this picture of a Gothic cathedral. How does it illustrate the power of the Catholic Church?

_____

_____

_____

_____

_____

PART B

Which labels for the Middle Ages best describe the era between 500 and 1400 in Europe: The Dark Ages, the Age of Feudalism, the Age of Faith, or the Golden Age of Europe? You must discuss three labels.

DBQ 4: TEACHER PAGE

Grading Key

Document 1

Anarchy dominated in Europe due to the barbarian attacks—the Moors in the South and the Hungarians in the East. Towns, villages, and churches were destroyed; there was no more trade; peasants were leaving their fields. It was the Dark Ages.

Document 2

In this feudal oath, John of Toul is promising his service and that of his knights.

Document 3

According to the *Anglo-Saxon Chronicle,* the Northmen were plundering and burning cities and taking captives back to their country. The Saracens, or Moors, were slaughtering Christians and taking prisoners.

Document 4

These are feudal obligations. The vassal promises his loyalty, military service, and ransom payment to his lord. In return, the lord promises his vassal that he will provide a fief and protection.

Document 5

In the Truce of God, the Catholic Church was trying to limit fighting on specific days. This is evidence of the power of the Church.

Document 6

This writer points out that during the Middle Ages the knowledge of the past was protected. Even more, the Middle Ages were "creative and inventive"—a Golden Age of sorts.

Document 7

This author believed that medieval culture ranked with that of earlier Golden Ages due to its philosophy, law, poetry, and architecture. Its greatest achievement, however, was the belief that service to others and to God is most important.

(continued)

Document 8

A monk promises to give up pleasures and possessions of this world. He takes vows of poverty, chastity, and purity, and promises to do service to God for his lifetime.

Document 9

In the Pope's call for a crusade, he was asking western Europeans to go to the aid of their fellow Christians in the Byzantine Empire who were under a fierce attack by the Arabs and Turks. The Pope demonstrated his power by stating that anyone who died on the crusade would have his sins forgiven.

Document 10

The spires of the Gothic cathedral point to heaven, the ultimate goal of the medieval man or woman. The cathedral was built to honor God. Its beautiful stained-glass windows, arches, flying buttresses, and sculptures illustrate the power of the Catholic Church.

Additional Information Beyond the Documents

The documents provide students with only fragments of evidence. Answers should include relevant information beyond the documents—information that students have learned from their classroom study. The following list suggests some of the information that students might include in the essay.

- Dark Ages—invasions, fall of Western Roman Empire

- Feudalism, manoral system, vassals, fiefs, nobles, serfs

- The many political, social, religious, and economic roles and power of the Catholic Church—sacraments, clergy, nuns, excommunication, teaching, tithing

- The art, architecture, and literary accomplishments of late Middle Ages, Gothic cathedrals, crusades

- Pope Urban II, vernacular

(continued)

Sample Student Essay

The Middle Ages, a period of time from the year 50 through 1400 B.C.E. have been referred to by a variety of terms including the Age of Faith, Feudalism, the Dark Ages, and a Golden Age. However, the three terms I believe describe this the most completely are the Age of Faith, Feudalism, and Golden Age.

Faith was an important aspect in medieval life. The Catholic Church was very powerful, for the clergy had influence on government as well as religion. Men of the church made laws of behavior for the people and helped the God-fearing Christians perform the sacraments, which ensured a place in heaven. The main goal for medieval citizens was to go to heaven, and the church controlled that decision of who was to go and who was not. If a certain person was found to be disobeying the rules of the church, he was excommunicated, and was shunned from the church, therefore ruining his chance to go to heaven. Even the king himself feared the power of God and the Pope. In addition many men and women became monks and nuns, proclaiming that they would ". . . renounce their own will for the will of God," and ". . . take the vows of purity, chastity, and poverty" (*Document 8*). The monks and nuns provided health care and religious education to the common people, therefore influencing medieval life.

The medieval period was also a feudal age. Social classes were rigid and strict, and one couldn't marry between them. The nobles were the upper class, the peasants and serfs the lower. Medieval lords would receive fiefs or pieces of land from a higher lord or the king himself. Eventually, this lord would distribute the land among other lower lords, called vassals. In return for the land, the vassals owed loyalty and military service. The lord promised protection from invaders to the vassal in addition to the land. Vassals usually had peasants or serfs working the land, and knights that provided military strength. Lords also had knights for protection. As stated in Document 2, vassals remained very loyal to their Lords; "I will aid the Count of Champagne . . . and will send knights whose service I owe to them for the fief which I hold of them." The manors that the feudalistic system originated were self-sufficient, for everything that was needed for survival was on this piece of land. A church for religion, fields to grow food, a mill for grinding, water from the well, and housing for the serfs in addition to the large manorhouse for the lord were all stationed in this one large area called the manor.

Lastly the Middle Ages were a Golden Age. In the later Middle Ages, there was a need for education and learning; the government needed more literate men for bureacracies, and the clergy requested a better education. Cathedrals which served as evidence of this Golden Age developed into the very first universities. In these schools, Europeans studied works of Aristotle, theology, and philosophy. Roman numerals were soon replaced by the easier to use Arabic number system. Medieval students also studied medicine and math, especially in the area of geometry. This ". . . age once described as 'dark' had . . . vitality and exuberance . . . they were

(continued)

creative and inventive" (*Document 6*). Literature written in the "vernacular" language, or common languages of French and Italian, started to be popular during the Middle Ages. A few examples are the *Divine Comedy* and *The Canterbury Tales*. Lastly, the building of the beautiful Gothic cathedrals with the high ceilings, stained-glass windows and flying buttresses were an example of the architectural feats of this time. As stated in Document 7, "It flourished in the midst of rude surroundings . . . we must judge them of their philosophy and law, poetry and architecture. (They) sprung from the soil and ripened in the atmosphere of a civilized society."

In conclusion, the Middle Ages was a time of many occurrences, but most certainly it was a time of faith, feudalism, and the thirst for knowledge.

Teacher Comments

This student essay thoroughly addresses all aspects of the task, identifying three labels that best describe the Middle Ages. It includes information from most of the documents as well as much relevant outside information, facts, and details. It weaves the documents in the body paragraphs and includes an introduction and conclusion. This is a well-organized, well-developed essay.

Score: 5

DBQ 5: BYZANTINE EMPIRE UNDER JUSTINIAN

Historical Context

When Justinian became emperor in 527, he was determined to revive the ancient Roman Empire, to build a new Rome. He established Constantinople as the capital of the Byzantine, or Eastern Roman, Empire. Justinian's actions preserved Roman heritage for more than a thousand years.

■ **Directions:** The following question is based on the accompanying documents in Part A. As you analyze the documents, take into account both the source of each document and the author's point of view. Be sure to do each of the following steps:

1. Carefully read the document-based question. Consider what you already know about this topic. How would you answer the question if you had no documents to examine?

2. Read each document carefully, underlining key phrases and words that address the document-based question. You may also wish to use the margin to make brief notes. Answer the questions that follow each document before moving on to the next document.

3. Based on your own knowledge and on the information found in the documents, formulate a thesis that directly answers the document-based question.

4. Organize supportive and relevant information into a brief outline.

5. Write a well-organized essay proving your thesis. You should present your essay logically. Include information both from the documents and from your own knowledge beyond the documents.

> **Question: Evaluate the reign of Emperor Justinian. Did Justinian revive the Roman Empire as the Byzantine Empire? What is his legacy?**

PART A The following documents deal with the reign of Justinian and the Byzantine Empire. Examine each document carefully. In the space provided, answer the questions that follow each document.

(continued)

DBQ 5: BYZANTINE EMPIRE UNDER JUSTINIAN

Document 1

In this adapted excerpt, Procopius describes Justininian.

Justinian created countless cities which did not exist before. And finding that the belief in God was . . . straying into errors . . . he . . . brought it about that it stood on the firm foundation of a single faith. Moreover, finding the laws obscure because they had become far more numerous than they should be, and in obvious confusion because they disagreed with each other, he preserved them [in the Code of Justinian, 529–534] . . . by controlling their discrepancies with the greatest firmness.

Source: Procopius, *Buildings*, Loeb Classical Library, 1940 (adapted)

According to Procopius, what were three contributions of Justinian?

_____

_____

_____

Document 2

Procopius also described Justinian in a different book, *The Secret History.*

Wisely, this book was published after Justinian's death. Justinian was . . . crafty, hypocritical, secretive by temperament, two-faced: a clever fellow with marvelous ability to conceal his real opinion . . . lying all the time. . . .

Source: Procopius, *The Secret History*, translated by Richard Atwater, 1927 (adapted)

Which characteristics of Justinian did Procopius stress in *The Secret History*?

_____

_____

_____

Why was this description so different from what Document 1 says about Justinian?

_____

_____

_____

(continued)

DBQ 5: BYZANTINE EMPIRE UNDER JUSTINIAN

Document 3

Justinian ruled like earlier Roman emperors. This is a description of him by a Byzantine official.

> The emperor is equal to all men in the nature of his body, but in the authority of his rank he is similar to God, who rules all.

How did this official explain Justinian's power?

_____

_____

Document 4

In this adapted excerpt, Procopius describes the Hagia Sophia, a magnificent church, upon its completion in 537.

> In height it rises to the very heavens. . . . A spherical-shaped dome . . . makes it exceedingly beautiful: from the lightness of the building it does not appear to rest upon a solid foundation, but to . . . be suspended from heaven by the fabled golden chain. . . . The entire ceiling is covered with pure gold, which adds glory to the beauty, though the rays of light reflected upon the gold from the marble surpass it in beauty. . . . And whenever anyone enters this church to pray, he understands at once that it is not by any human strength or skill, but by the influence of God, that this work has been perfected. And so his mind is lifted up toward God. . . . Moreover, it is impossible to describe the treasure of gold and silver plate and gems, which the Emperor Justinian has presented to it. . . .

What were the distinctive characteristics of the Hagia Sophia?

_____

_____

What impact did the church have on a visitor?

_____

_____

(continued)

DBQ 5: BYZANTINE EMPIRE UNDER JUSTINIAN

Document 5

Justinian was a great builder. This is evident from the fortifications and buildings he constructed in Constantinople, shown on the map below.

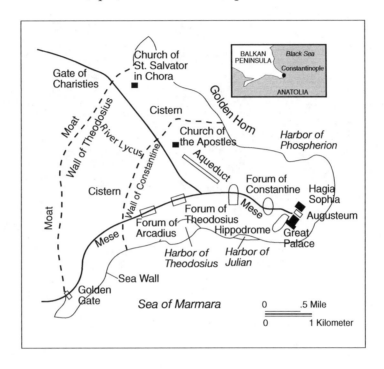

Study this map and describe the building projects that made Constantinople the center of power. In addition, discuss Constantinople's strategic location for trade and defense.

_____

_____

_____

_____

_____

_____

_____

_____

_____

(continued)

DBQ 5: BYZANTINE EMPIRE UNDER JUSTINIAN

Document 6

The Byzantine Empire reached its greatest size under Justinian. From 565 until the empire's collapse in 1453, several invaders took sections of it.

The Byzantine Empire in 527

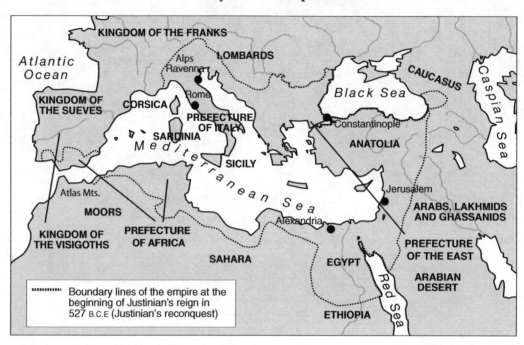

What areas were included in the Byzantine Empire?

_____

_____

What problems did Justinian's reconquests cause for the empire?

_____

_____

PART B Evaluate the reign of Emperor Justinian. Did Justinian revive the Roman Empire as the Byzantine Empire? What is his legacy?

DBQ 5: TEACHER PAGE

Grading Key

Document 1

Justinian built cities; he restored the Byzantine Empire to one faith; he organized a uniform legal code.

Document 2

Procopius described Justinian as a liar and a hypocrite. In the first excerpt, Procopius wrote as the official historian for Justinian. In *The Secret History,* Procopius gave his personal, and perhaps more honest, description.

Document 3

Justinian ruled with absolute power, as he was "similar to God."

Document 4

The Hagia Sophia was noteworthy because of its height—it "rises to the very heavens." It was topped with a beautiful spherical dome. Inside, the light reflected the gold that covered the ceiling. There was a feeling of light and beauty throughout the huge church. Consequently, a visitor felt that this was a work built with the "influence of God" and thus raised one's attention "up toward God."

Document 5

This map shows Constantinople's location on the Sea of Marmara, part of the waterway system that connects the Black Sea and the Aegean Sea. Its location made Constantinople a center of trade for goods coming from Asia, Africa, and Europe. As for defense, Constantinople was surrounded on three sides by water, which protected it from attack. It also had a moat, the Wall of Theodosius, and the Wall of Constantine as fortifications on its west side. In addition to the walls that were built for protection, Justinian rebuilt Hagia Sophia, enlarged the palace, built roads and aqueducts, and provided entertainment in the Hippodrome. All of these projects demonstrated the power of the emperor and of the Byzantine Empire.

Document 6

The Byzantine Empire, with Constantinople as its capital, included Asia Minor, the Balkans, Greece, Italy, Egypt, and the coasts of North Africa and southern Spain. The cost of regaining parts of the empire and protecting it from attacks left the treasury depleted.

(continued)

Additional Information Beyond the Documents

These documents provide students with only fragments of evidence. Essays should include relevant information beyond the documents—information that students have learned from their classroom study. The following list suggests some of the information from their outside learning that students might include in their essays.

- Extent of Roman Empire and its legacy—law, engineering, literature, history

- Justinian's Code

- Fortification of Constantinople

- Hagia Sophia

- Preserved Greek and Roman works—philosophy, literature, math, and history, as well as contributions mentioned in the documents

DBQ 6: ISLAMIC CIVILIZATION: ITS CONTRIBUTIONS TO WORLD CULTURE

Historical Context

The Muslims inherited much from Greece, Rome, and India. They also adopted much from the people they conquered. Because of their tolerance of other cultures, the Muslims were able to advance scholarship in several areas to the highest level of that time. As a result, Muslim achievements stand out and have a lasting impact on world cultures.

■ **Directions:** The following question is based on the accompanying documents in Part A. As you analyze the documents, take into account both the source of each document and the author's point of view. Be sure to do each of the following steps:

1. Carefully read the document-based question. Consider what you already know about this topic. How would you answer the question if you had no documents to examine?

2. Read each document carefully, underlining key phrases and words that address the document-based question. You may also wish to use the margin to make brief notes. Answer the questions that follow each document before moving on to the next document.

3. Based on your own knowledge and on the information found in the documents, formulate a thesis that directly answers the document-based question.

4. Organize supportive and relevant information into a brief outline.

5. Write a well-organized essay proving your thesis. You should present your essay logically. Include information both from the documents and from your own knowledge beyond the documents.

Question: What were the most important Islamic achievements? Why were the Muslims able to make such great contributions, and how did these contributions impact the world?

  The following documents will help you understand Islamic achievements. Examine each document carefully. In the space provided, answer the question or questions that follow each document.

(continued)

DBQ 6: ISLAMIC CIVILIZATION: ITS CONTRIBUTIONS TO WORLD CULTURE

Document 1

This document explains why Muslims of the Islamic Empire both preserved existing knowledge and extended it.

> Muslims had practical reasons for supporting the advancement of science. Rulers wanted qualified physicians treating their ills. The faithful . . . relied on mathematicians and astronomers to calculate the times for prayer and the direction of Mecca. . . . Their attitude reflected a deep-seated curiosity about the world and a quest for truth that reached back as far as . . . Mohammed himself.
>
> After the fall of Rome in 476 B.C.E., Europe entered a period of upheaval and chaos, an era in which scholarship suffered. . . . In the early 800s, Caliph al-Ma'mun opened in Baghdad . . . the House of Wisdom. There, scholars of different cultures and beliefs worked . . . translating texts from Greece, India, Persia, and elsewhere into Arabic.

Source: Bech, Black, Krieger, Naylor, Shabaka, *World History: Patterns of Interaction,* McDougal Littell, 1999 (adapted)

What were the reasons for Muslims' interest in learning at this time in history?

_____

_____

_____

Document 2

The Islamic capital of Cordova (in present-day Spain) was described by a contemporary as the "jewel of the world." European scholars preferred Cordova's Islamic schools and universities over other study sources in Europe.

> Besides the university library, Arab statisticians assure us the city boasted 37 libraries, numberless bookstores, 800 public schools . . . and a total population of 300,000. Its people enjoyed a high standard of living and refinement and walked on paved streets . . . all this at a time when hardly a town in Europe, Constantinople excepted, counted more than a few thousand inhabitants. Parisians and Londoners were still trudging on muddy, dark alleys.

Source: Philip Hitti, *Capital Cities of Arab Islam,* University of Minnesota Press, 1973 (adapted)

(continued)

DBQ 6: ISLAMIC CIVILIZATION: ITS CONTRIBUTIONS TO WORLD CULTURE

What conditions in Cordova did this author cite as evidence of the high level of Islamic civilization and scholarship?

_____

_____

_____

Document 3

Physician al-Razi wrote a medical reference encyclopedia, the *Comprehensive Book*. He also wrote *Treatise on Smallpox and Measles*. Ibn Sina (Avicenna) wrote the five-volume *The Canon of Medicine*. These books were translated into Latin and other languages and influenced doctors in Europe. This document describes the influence of these Islamic books on European medicine.

Medical Reference Books

When Europeans learned that Muslims had preserved important medical texts, they wanted to translate the texts into Latin. In the 11th century, scholars traveled to libraries in places such as Toledo, Spain, where they began translating—but only after they learned to read Arabic.

Through this process, European medical schools gained access to vital reference sources such as al-Razi's *Comprehensive Book* and Ibn Sina's *The Canon of Medicine*. Ibn Sina's five-volume encyclopedia guided doctors of Europe and Southwest Asia for six centuries. For nearly 500 years, al-Qasim's work, *The Method,* which contained original drawings of some 200 medical tools, was the foremost textbook on surgery in Europe.

Source: Bech, Black, Krieger, Naylor, Shabaka, *World History: Patterns of Interaction,* McDougal Littell, 1999 (adapted)

What does this document tell you about Muslim medical knowledge at this time in history?

_____

_____

How did it impact Western civilization?

_____

_____

(continued)

DBQ 6: ISLAMIC CIVILIZATION: ITS CONTRIBUTIONS TO WORLD CULTURE

Document 4

Al-Khwarizmi, a Muslim mathematician, studied Indian sources. He wrote a textbook in the 800s about *al-jabr* (the Arabic word for what we call "algebra" today). This book was later translated into Latin and used throughout Europe. Muslim mathematicians also adopted Arabic numerals from the Indians and used them in a place-value system. Here are examples of these two advances:

$$3x = 15 \qquad \begin{array}{r} 135 \\ +20 \\ \hline 155 \end{array}$$

What was the importance of these mathematical advances?

_____

_____

How did these developments impact Western civilization?

_____

_____

Document 5

Muslim scholars also made advances in trigonometry, astronomy, and mapmaking. To do so, they relied on scientific observation and their understanding of mathematics and optics. They used the astrolabe (Figure A) and the armillary sphere (Figure B) to study the skies and make calculations for their calendars and maps.

Figure A

Figure B

(continued)

DBQ 6: ISLAMIC CIVILIZATION: ITS CONTRIBUTIONS TO WORLD CULTURE

How did each of these instruments impact Muslim and Western civilization?

_____

_____

_____

Document 6

Muslim artists used calligraphy to decorate buildings and objects of art as well as to reflect the glory of Allah. Study this example.

Why did Muslims use calligraphy in religious art?

_____

_____

What impact has calligraphy had on world art?

_____

_____

_____

(continued)

Document-Based Assessment for
Global History

DBQ 6: ISLAMIC CIVILIZATION: ITS CONTRIBUTIONS TO WORLD CULTURE

Document 7

Muslim architects blended features from various sources, including the Byzantine Empire, and also added new features. Study this photograph of the Dome of the Rock in Jerusalem.

What are the distinctive architectural features of this building?

_____

_____

What impact did these architectural features have on buildings throughout the world?

_____

_____

Document 8

The standard for Arabic literature and poetry is the Quran, which influenced Sufi poets. These lines are from the Quran and from a Sufi poem.

> In the name of the Merciful and Compassionate Allah. That is the Book! There is no doubt therein. . . . Allah, there is no Allah but He! He will surely assemble you on the resurrection day.
>
> —Quran
>
> As salt resolved in the ocean was swallowed in Allah's sea. . . .
>
> —Jalal al-Din Rumi, *Persian Poems*

Source: Quran; Jalal al-Din Rumi, *Persian Poems*, thirteenth century (adapted)

(continued)

DBQ 6: ISLAMIC CIVILIZATION: ITS CONTRIBUTIONS TO WORLD CULTURE

Why is the Quran the model for poetry?

_____

_____

_____

How did the Quran influence literature and poetry?

_____

_____

_____

Document 9

Between 750 and 1350, Muslim merchants built a trade network throughout their empire.

> Masters of the sea, even as of the land, the Arabs spread throughout the geographical area. The whole world was theirs to explore . . . their ships sailed across the seas even as they moved across the land [Sahara Desert into West Africa]. The might of the sword of Islam carved the way for the slaveowner and the merchant to follow.

Source: Sir T.H. Holdich, *The Gates of India*, MacMillan, 1910 (adapted)

Why and where were the Muslims able to establish a trading empire?

_____

_____

_____

_____

(continued)

DBQ 6: ISLAMIC CIVILIZATION: ITS CONTRIBUTIONS TO WORLD CULTURE

Document 10

This adapted excerpt describes the benefits that Europeans received from Muslim industry.

> First should be mentioned the textile products imported from Islamic countries: muslin . . . damask . . . gauze, cotton, satin.
>
> Natural products, which by their name indicate they were imported from Islamic countries—fruits, like orange, lemon, and apricot; vegetables, like spinach, artichokes, and saffron. . . . Finally our commercial vocabulary itself has preserved . . . proofs that there was a time when Islamic trade and trade customs exercised a deep influence on the commercial development of Christian countries—such words as "traffic" [derived from Arabic *tafriq*], which means distribution.

Source: J.H. Kramers, *The Legacy of Islam*, Clarendon Press, 1931 (adapted)

What were the commercial or trade benefits that Europeans gained from Islamic commerce and industry?

_____

_____

_____

PART B   What were the most important Islamic achievements? Why were the Muslims able to make such great contributions, and how did these contributions impact the world?

DBQ 6: TEACHER PAGE

Grading Key

Document 1

Rulers wanted skilled medical care. As Muslims, people needed to know the direction of Mecca from where they were and the times for daily prayer. They were curious about this world in much the same way Mohammed was. The Muslim Empire became a center of learning because, after the fall of Rome, there was chaos in Europe. At the same time, Muslim rulers encouraged scholars to translate books into Arabic.

Document 2

Cordova was a center of learning for its inhabitants. They enjoyed the necessities of life and a number of comforts that allowed for time to pursue learning in many fields.

Document 3

Muslims knew a lot about diseases and medical procedures. They were more advanced than the Europeans, who gained much knowledge from Muslim medical texts.

Document 4

Neither algebra nor "Arabic" numerals had been known in Europe before this time. The "Arabic" numeral system was easier to use than Roman numerals. Muslims' work in algebra was translated and used throughout Europe.

Document 5

The astrolabe was used to measure the angles of the sun and stars. By lining up the top rings of the armillary sphere, astronomers could calculate the time of day or year. This information was used in mapmaking and for calendars.

Document 6

Calligraphy was used to glorify Allah. Since the Quran forbade the depicting of living beings, Muslims used calligraphy in decorative arts in their mosques, and on glass, ceramic, woodwork, and books. This feature inspired its use in other world art.

Document 7

The gold dome and arches are important features of this mosque, as are mosaic art and calligraphy. All these features became seen in mosques around the world.

(continued)

Document 8

The Quran is sacred to Muslims. It contains praise of Allah and Islam. The influence of Allah can be seen in the poem.

Document 9

Muslims traded on land and sea. They controlled land along the Mediterranean Sea and were able to cross the Sahara Desert with their camel caravans. As they spread their religion and conquered and expanded their empire, they created a trading network.

Document 10

As a result of trading with the Islamic merchants, Europeans acquired textiles, fruits, vegetables, and even new vocabulary.

Additional Information Beyond the Documents

These documents provide students with only fragments of evidence. Essays should include relevant information beyond the documents—information that students have learned from their classroom study. The following list suggests some of the information from their outside learning that students might include in their essays.

- Islamic beliefs and practices

- Islamic achievements in medicine, math, science, calligraphy, literature, and architecture

- The civilizations and cultures included in the Islamic Empire—for example, India and North Africa—and trade

DBQ 7: AFRICA BEFORE EUROPEAN ARRIVAL

Historical Context

Africans had developed advanced civilizations before the Europeans arrived in the fifteenth and sixteenth centuries. Several centers of advanced civilization existed in Africa between 300 and 1400. The kingdom of Aksum (Ethiopia today) arose in East Africa. It flourished beginning in the 300s. Other African kingdoms, empires, and cities also arose and declined. In West Africa, three empires—Ghana, Mali, and Songhai—became wealthy and powerful by controlling the gold and salt trade. Between 1000 and 1500, cities on Africa's east coast also gained wealth and power through trade.

■ **Directions:** The following question is based on the accompanying documents in Part A. As you analyze the documents, take into account both the source of each document and the author's point of view. Be sure to do each of the following steps:

1. Carefully read the document-based question. Consider what you already know about this topic. How would you answer the question if you had no documents to examine?

2. Read each document carefully, underlining key phrases and words that address the document-based question. You may also wish to use the margin to make brief notes. Answer the questions that follow each document before moving on to the next document.

3. Based on your own knowledge and on the information found in the documents, formulate a thesis that directly answers the document-based question.

4. Organize supportive and relevant information into a brief outline.

5. Write a well-organized essay proving your thesis. You should present your essay logically. Include information both from the documents and from your own knowledge beyond the documents.

> **Question: What were the achievements of the African empires, kingdoms, and cities before the arrival of the Europeans? Explain and evaluate these achievements.**

PART A   The following documents provide information about African cultures before European arrival. Examine each document carefully. In the space provided, answer the questions that follow each document.

(continued)

DBQ 7: AFRICA BEFORE EUROPEAN ARRIVAL

Document 1

Aksum reached its height between 325 and 360. Aksum's location made it an important international trading center. This map shows the trade routes to and from Aksum between 300 and 700.

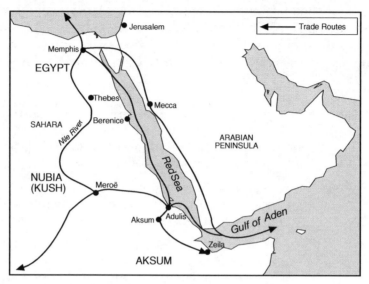

How did Aksum's location enable it to become a trading center?

_____

_____

_____

Document 2

Between 800 and 1076, the kingdom of Ghana was rich and powerful. It controlled the trans-Saharan gold and salt trade. This document describes the king's court in ancient Ghana. It was written by the Arab scholar Al-Bakri in 1067.

> The court of appeal is held in a domed pavilion around which stand ten horses with gold embroidered trappings. Behind the king stand ten pages holding shields and swords decorated with gold, and on his right are the sons of the subordinate kings of his country, all wearing splendid garments and with their hair mixed with gold. The governor of the city sits on the ground before the king, and around him are ministers seated likewise. At the door of the pavilion are dogs . . . [wearing] collars of gold and silver, studded with a number of balls of the same metals.

Source: Leon E. Clark, editor, *Through African Eyes,* Praeger Press, Inc., 1970 (adapted)

(continued)

DBQ 7: AFRICA BEFORE EUROPEAN ARRIVAL

What evidence of wealth did Al-Bakri describe?

_____

_____

_____

What evidence of an advanced political structure did Al-Bakri describe?

_____

_____

_____

Document 3

The following excerpt is an explanation for the wealth of the kingdom of Ghana.

> The Arab traders of this region wanted gold as much as the Wangara wanted salt, but both had to pass through Ghana to trade. . . . Ghana controlled the land . . . [and] it had the military forces . . . to maintain peace in the area, thereby assuring safe trade for the Arabs and the Wangara.
>
> Ancient Ghana was an extremely complex empire. It possessed many of the characteristics of powerful nations today: wealth based on trade, sufficient food to feed its people, income derived from taxes, social organization that ensured justice and efficient political control, a strong army equipped with advanced weapons, and a foreign policy that led to peace and cooperation with other people.

Source: Leon E. Clark, editor, *Through African Eyes*, Praeger Press, Inc., 1970 (adapted)

What was ancient Ghana's role in the gold-salt trade?

_____

_____

What characteristics of an advanced civilization did ancient Ghana possess?

_____

_____

_____

(continued)

DBQ 7: AFRICA BEFORE EUROPEAN ARRIVAL

Document 4

Mansa Musa expanded the Mali empire to twice the size of the Ghana empire it replaced. On his hajj to Mecca in 1324–25, Mansa Musa stopped in Cairo, Egypt. An Egyptian official described him.

> This man, Mansa Musa, spread upon Cairo the flood of his generosity: there was no person, officer of the court, or holder of any office of the Sultanate who did not receive a sum of gold from him.

What about Mansa Musa impressed the Egyptian official?

_____

_____

_____

Document 5

In this excerpt, a Moroccan traveler using the name Leo Africanus describes the city of Timbuktu in West Africa.

> Here are many doctors, judges, priests, and other learned men that are well maintained at the king's costs. Various manuscripts and written books are brought here . . . and sold for more money than other merchandise.

Source: Leo Africanus, "The Description of Africa (1526)," *Reading About the World,* *Volume 2,* Harcourt Brace Custom Publishers, 1999 (adapted)

What about Timbuktu impressed this writer?

_____

_____

_____

(continued)

56

DBQ 7: AFRICA BEFORE EUROPEAN ARRIVAL

Document 6

Ibn Battuta traveled in Mali in 1352. In this adapted excerpt, he describes his travels.

> They are seldom unjust, and have a greater abhorrence [hatred] of injustice than any other people. Their sultan shows no mercy to anyone who is guilty of the least act of it. There is complete security in their country. Neither traveler nor inhabitant in it has anything to fear from robbers.

Source: Ibn Battuta, *Travels in Asia and Africa 1325-1354*, tr. and ed. H.A.R. Gibb, Broadway House, 1929 (adapted)

What two things impressed Ibn Battuta about Mali?

_____

_____

_____

Document 7

This description of the lost-wax process of making bronze sculpture comes from an oral account of a Hausa artisan.

> In the name of Allah the Compassionate, the Merciful. This account will show how the [Benin] figures are made. This work is one to cause wonder. Now this kind of work is done with clay, and wax, and red metal [copper], and solder [zinc], and lead, and fire. . . . Next it is set aside to cool, then [the outside covering of clay] is broken off. Then you see a beautiful figure. . . .

Source: Henry Balfour, "Modern Brass-Casting in West Africa," *The Journal of the Royal Anthropological Institute of Great Britain and Ireland*, Vol. 40, 1910 (adapted)

Why is this bronze statue described as a "wonder"?

_____

_____

_____

(continued)

DBQ 7: AFRICA BEFORE EUROPEAN ARRIVAL

Document 8

Ibn Battuta also visited Kilwa, an East African coastal city-state, in 1331. He described it as one of the most beautiful cities in the world. He admired the luxury enjoyed by the Muslim rulers and merchants. Kilwa controlled the overseas trade between the interior of Africa and sites around that part of the world. This map shows East African trade routes in 1000.

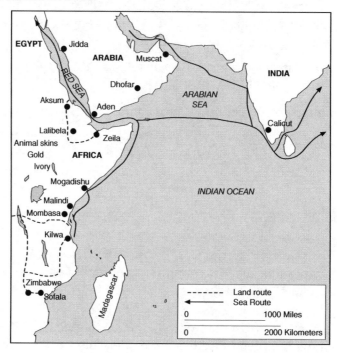

What sea routes was Kilwa connected to? What geographical areas did these sea routes lead to?

_____

_____

_____

What products were brought from the interior of Africa to Kilwa by the land route?

_____

_____

PART B What were the achievements of the African empires, kingdoms, and cities before the arrival of the Europeans? Explain and evaluate these achievements.

Grading Key

Document 1

Aksum's location on the Red Sea provided it with an extensive coastline and ports, and access to the countries on both the Mediterranean Sea and the Indian Ocean. Therefore, Aksum traded with India, Greek and Roman cities, and areas in the Far East. The caravan routes connected Aksum to Egypt and to the interior of Africa.

Document 2

The wealth of Ghana was evident in the gold in the horses' equipment and the shields of the pages, and the gold and silver in the collars of the dogs. The advanced political system was evident in the organization the king assembled—the governor and ministers.

Document 3

Since Ghana had no gold or salt, it controlled the land and maintained peace so that trade was safe. The characteristics of an advanced civilization included ample food supplies; money to provide a strong, well-equipped army; and an efficient government.

Document 4

He was impressed with the amount of gold that Mansa Musa had and with his willingness to give it away.

Document 5

He saw Timbuktu as a center of "learned men" who were supported by the king. Books were highly valued there.

Document 6

Ibn Battuta was impressed with the justice and security enjoyed by all the people of Mali.

Document 7

The bronze statue was produced using molten metals and the wax displacement process. The statue was very detailed.

(continued)

Document 8

The sea routes connected Kilwa to the Red Sea, the Indian Ocean, and the Arabian Sea. As a result, Kilwa was connected to sites in the Arabian peninsula, India, and the Far East, as well as other sites along the African coast. The products brought from the interior of Africa included gold, ivory, and animal skins.

Additional Information Beyond the Documents

These documents provide students with only fragments of evidence. Essays should include relevant information from beyond the documents—information that students have learned from their classroom study. The following list suggests some of the information from their outside learning that students might want to include in their essays.

- Trade patterns and products in West Africa and East Africa

- Art and architecture of each kingdom and empire—Aksum, Ghana, Mali, Songhai

- Governmental organization

- Learning, language, and belief systems

- Cultural diffusion and blending

DBQ 8: CIVILIZATIONS OF THE AMERICAS

Historical Context

   Between 300 and 1500, three advanced civilizations developed in Central and South America. The Mayas flourished from 250 to 900. Mayan ruins remain even today in Central America. The Aztecs conquered most of Mexico. They built a highly developed civilization in the 1400s. At the same time, the Incas were building an empire in Peru.

■ **Directions:** The following question is based on the accompanying documents in Part A. As you analyze the documents, take into account both the source of each document and the author's point of view. Be sure to do each of the following steps:

   1. Carefully read the document-based question. Consider what you already know about this topic. How would you answer the question if you had no documents to examine?

   2. Read each document carefully, underlining key phrases and words that address the document-based question. You may also wish to use the margin to make brief notes. Answer the questions that follow each document before moving on to the next document.

   3. Based on your own knowledge and on the information found in the documents, formulate a thesis that directly answers the document-based question.

   4. Organize supportive and relevant information into a brief outline.

   5. Write a well-organized essay proving your thesis. You should present your essay logically. Include information both from the documents and from your own knowledge beyond the documents.

> **Question: How advanced were the Mayan, Aztec, and Incan civilizations? What were their major accomplishments?**

 PART A   The following documents deal with the former civilizations of Central and South America. Examine each document carefully. In the space provided, answer the questions that follow each document.

(continued)

DBQ 8: CIVILIZATIONS OF THE AMERICAS

Document 1

This Mayan pyramid temple in Tikal was the tallest structure in the Americas until the twentieth century.

Describe the significance of Mayan architecture evidenced in this temple at Tikal.

_____

_____

_____

Document 2

This is a glyph (symbol) from the Mayan calendar.

What is the significance of this glyph? _____

_____

_____

_____

(continued)

DBQ 8: CIVILIZATIONS OF THE AMERICAS

Document 3

When he arrived in 1519, the Spanish conqueror Hernán Cortés was awed by the magnificent Aztec capital of Tenochtitlán. He wrote a letter to King Charles of Spain describing the city.

> The city has many squares where markets are held and trading is carried on. There is one square . . . where there are daily more than 60,000 souls, buying and selling, and where are found all the kinds of merchandise produced in these countries, including food products, jewels of gold and silver, lead, brass, copper, zinc, bones, shells, and feathers.

Why was Cortés impressed when he arrived in Tenochtitlán in 1519?

_____

_____

_____

Document 4

This description of farming in the Incan empire in 1539 was written by Garcilasco de la Vega. He was the son of an Incan princess and a Spanish explorer.

> As soon as the Incan ruler had conquered any kingdom and set up his government, he ordered that the farmland used to grow corn be extended. For this purpose, he ordered irrigation channels to be constructed. The engineers showed great cleverness and skill in supplying water for the crops, since only scattered sections of the land could grow corn. For this reason, they endeavored to increase its fertility as much as possible.

What engineering technique did de la Vega describe?

_____

_____

Why was this a significant achievement?

_____

_____

_____

(continued)

DBQ 8: CIVILIZATIONS OF THE AMERICAS

Document 5

This map shows the Incan empire in 1565.

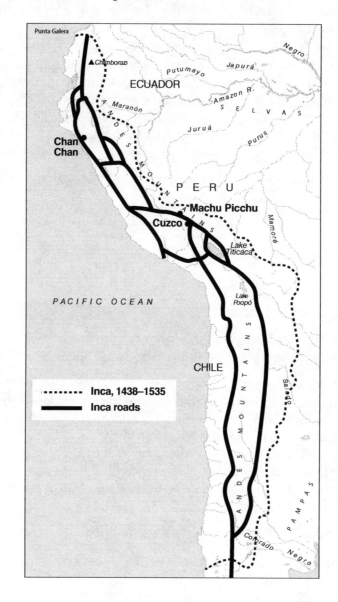

How did the Incan government unite its empire in the Andes Mountains?

_____

_____

_____

(continued)

DBQ 8: CIVILIZATIONS OF THE AMERICAS

What is the significance of this accomplishment?

_____

_____

_____

Document 6

This photograph of the ruins of Machu Picchu provides evidence of the superior building design and farming techniques of the Incas in Peru.

What specific farming and building techniques did the Incas use?

_____

_____

_____

_____

_____

PART B How advanced were the Mayan, Aztec, and Incan civilizations? What were their major accomplishments?

Grading Key

Document 1

This pyramid temple is evidence of the architectural skills of the Mayas. They were able to build monumental temples of stone, which they dedicated to both the gods and important rulers.

Document 2

This hieroglyphic symbol, or glyph, is part of the advanced writing system of the ancient Mayas. The Mayas used this writing system to record important historical events in stone.

Document 3

Tenochtitlán was a bustling city, a market center where foods and all kinds of merchandise were bought and sold. This impressed Cortés a great deal.

Document 4

Incan engineers developed an extensive irrigation system. This made it possible to grow corn and other crops on land that otherwise would not have been productive. The irrigation system made it possible to feed the people of the extensive Incan empire.

Document 5

The map shows the roads that the Incas constructed to unite the people throughout the empire. Great engineering skills were involved in building roads, bridges, tunnels, and steps to cross rivers and mountains. The Incas built one of the greatest road systems in the world.

Document 6

The ruins of Machu Picchu, the Incan city built by the Incas in the Andes Mountains, remain today as evidence of the great building skills of the Incas. They fitted stones together without mortar and built houses that have survived earthquakes for centuries. They terraced mountainsides to increase the farmland available to grow crops.

(continued)

Additional Information Beyond the Documents

These documents provide students with only fragments of evidence. Essays should include relevant information beyond just the documents—information that students have learned from their classroom study. The following list suggests some of the information from their outside learning that students might include in their essays.

Mayas	Incas	Aztecs
Mexico	Peru	Mesoamerica, Mexico
Central America	sun-god king	pyramid builders
Palenque	religion—multiple gods	city builders
city-state	government—centralized	religion—many gods
religion—many gods	united—common language	government—king
writing system	engineers—roads, bridges	pictorial written language
mathematics, astronomy, calendars		trade
farming and trading		calendars

DBQ 9: TRADE AND INTERACTION

Historical Context

Trade, conquest, and warfare have impacted peoples around the world throughout history. These interactions have changed the cultures of the societies involved in positive and negative ways.

■ **Directions:** The following question is based on the accompanying documents in Part A. As you analyze the documents, take into account both the source of each document and the author's point of view. Be sure to do each of the following steps:

1. Carefully read the document-based question. Consider what you already know about this topic. How would you answer the question if you had no documents to examine?

2. Read each document carefully, underlining key phrases and words that address the document-based question. You may also wish to use the margin to make brief notes. Answer the questions that follow each document before moving on to the next document.

3. Based on your own knowledge and on the information found in the documents, formulate a thesis that directly answers the document-based question.

4. Organize supportive and relevant information into a brief outline.

5. Write a well-organized essay proving your thesis. You should present your essay logically. Include information both from the documents and from your own knowledge beyond the documents.

> **Question: Choose two world regions (China, Africa, Europe, the Middle East, or the Americas). How did trade have positive and/or negative effects on the people in two of those regions?**

PART A The following documents deal with trading interactions among various world regions. Examine each document carefully. In the space provided, answer the questions that follow each document.

(continued)

DBQ 9: TRADE AND INTERACTION

Document 1

The map below shows overland trade routes across Asia. These routes became heavily used in the centuries after 300 C.E. The overall route was known as the Silk Road. China exported its silk, iron, and bronze. Merchants took these goods west to the Middle East and then to Europe. Gold, glass, ivory, animal hides, horses, and cattle were brought east to China from the Middle East and Central Asia. Trade contacts with India led to the introduction of Buddhism to China.

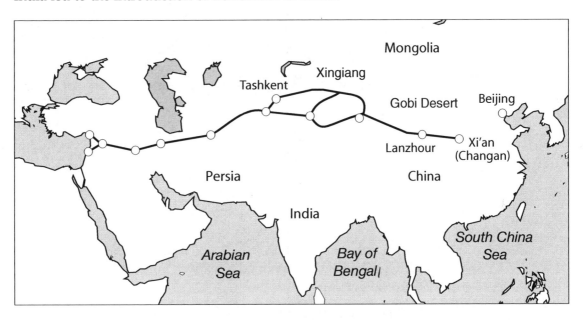

What products were taken from China to the Middle East (Southwest Asia) along the Silk Road, and then on to Europe?

_____

_____

What products and ideas were taken to China along the Silk Road?

_____

_____

What impact did the Silk Road have on the people of Europe and Asia?

_____

_____

_____

(continued)

DBQ 9: TRADE AND INTERACTION

Document 2

The map below shows the voyages of Zheng He, a Chinese admiral, in the 1400s.

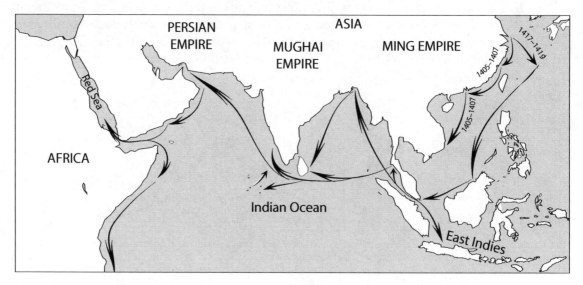

This excerpt comments on the impact of Zheng He's voyages.

> Yonglo [the Ming ruler] hoped to impress the world with the power and splendor of Ming China and also hoped to expand China's tribute system. Zheng He's voyages accomplished these goals. . . .
>
> Everywhere Zheng He went, he distributed gifts, such as gold, silver, silk, and scented oils, to show Chinese superiority. As a result, more than 16 countries sent tribute to the Ming court. Many envoys traveled to China. . . .
>
> Demand for Chinese goods had a ripple effect on the economy. Industries such as silk making and ceramics grew rapidly. Manufacturing and commerce increased. However, China did not become highly industrialized for two main reasons. First, the whole idea of commerce offended China's Confucian beliefs. . . . Second, Chinese economic policies traditionally favored agriculture. Taxes on agriculture stayed low. Taxes on manufacturing and trade skyrocketed.

Source: Bech, Black, Krieger, Naylor, Shabaka, *World History: Patterns of Interaction*, McDougal Littell, 1999 (adapted)

Where did Zheng He's voyages go?

_____

_____

(continued)

DBQ 9: TRADE AND INTERACTION

How did China benefit from the voyages of Zheng He?

_____

_____

_____

Document 3

The text below discusses the effects of the Crusades.

> The Crusades caused a growth in trade between Europe and the Middle East. European demand for the products of Southwest Asia grew greatly. Products such as spices, sugar, lemons, rugs, glass, perfumes, and silk and cotton textiles flowed into Europe. This increased trade had several effects, including the following:
>
> - Increased wealth and power for the Italian city-states that controlled trade with the Middle East
>
> - New ideas and learning gained by Europeans from contact with Muslims
>
> - Rediscovery in Europe of the writings of ancient Greeks and Romans, preserved by Muslim scholars; this later encouraged the Renaissance
>
> - Growth of intolerance as Christians persecuted Jews and Muslims in Europe and Muslims persecuted Christians in Europe

How did Europe benefit from the Crusades? List two benefits.

_____

_____

_____

What were negative effects of the Crusades on people in Europe and the Middle East?

_____

_____

_____

(continued)

DBQ 9: TRADE AND INTERACTION

Document 4

The map below shows trade routes to and through Europe in the thirteenth to fifteenth centuries.

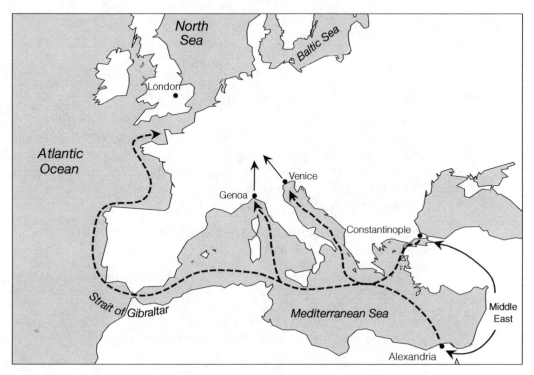

According to the map, where did the trade routes originate? _____

_____

Why were the Italian city-states able to dominate the trade patterns at this time?

_____

_____

_____

What was the impact of these trade routes on Italian city-states and on the place of origin?

_____

_____

_____

_____

(continued)

DBQ 9: TRADE AND INTERACTION

Document 5

The illustration below shows the Columbian Exchange.

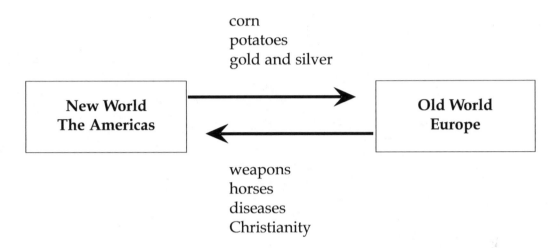

corn
potatoes
gold and silver

New World
The Americas

Old World
Europe

weapons
horses
diseases
Christianity

According to this diagram, what were the positive and negative impacts of the exchange on both the Americans and the Europeans?

_____

_____

_____

_____

_____

(continued)

DBQ 9: TRADE AND INTERACTION

Document 6

The map below shows the trade pattern of the Atlantic economy in the eighteenth century.

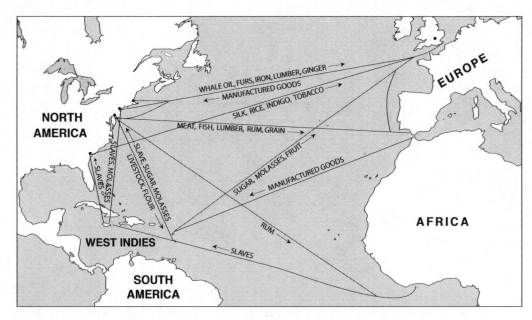

What were the benefits to Europe of this eighteenth-century trade pattern?

_____

_____

_____

What was the negative impact of the trade pattern on Africa?

_____

_____

_____

PART B Choose two world regions (China, Africa, Europe, the Middle East, or the Americas). How did trade have positive and/or negative effects on the people in two of those regions?

DBQ 9: TEACHER PAGE

Grading Key

Document 1

China sent silk, iron, and bronze to the Middle East and Europe. China got gold, glass, ivory, animal hides, horses, and cattle, as well as Buddhism. People along the Silk Road shared ideas and goods that were new to them. Trade flourished along the Silk Road.

Document 2

Zheng He traveled from China along the coasts of Southeast Asia, South Asia, Southwest Asia, and Africa. Demand in these areas for Chinese goods increased. As a result, manufacturing (of silk and ceramics, for example) and commerce grew. Also, China received tribute from many of the nations that Zheng He visited.

Document 3

Benefits included the following:

1. Increased trade with the Middle East, involving the products of Southwest Asia such as spices, sugar, rugs, perfumes, and silk and cotton textiles

2. Exposure to Muslim learning and ideas

3. European rediscovery of early Greek and Roman learning, a factor in the development of the Renaissance

A negative effect of the Crusades was a growth of intolerance as Christians persecuted Jews and Muslims in Europe and Muslims persecuted Christians in Europe.

Document 4

Trade originated in the Middle East. Italian city-states were located on the Mediterranean Sea and used their ships to carry goods from the Middle East to ports with access to land routes. Italian city-states grew in wealth and power, so they became leaders during the Renaissance. The Middle East also grew in wealth.

Document 5

Europeans attained corn, potatoes, gold, and silver from the New World, with no negative effects. The Americans attained weapons, horses, and Christianity. One negative effect was the introduction of diseases that killed many Americans.

(continued)

Document 6

Europe gained raw materials such as furs, iron, lumber, rice, tobacco, sugar, molasses, and fruit, as well as markets for European manufactured goods. The slave trade sent enslaved Africans to the Americas, largely to work on plantations.

Additional Information Beyond the Documents

These documents provide students with only fragments of evidence. Essays should include relevant information beyond the documents—information that students have learned from their classroom study, outside reading and viewing, and other learning experiences. The following list suggests some of the information from their outside learning that students might include in their essays.

- The Silk Road and the products that were traded

- Chinese history and trade in the fifteenth century

- Results of the Crusades

- The results of Spanish colonization of the New World

- Trade patterns that developed during colonization

DBQ 10: CAUSES OF THE FRENCH REVOLUTION

Historical Context

The French Revolution of 1789 had many long-range causes. Political, social, and economic conditions in France made many French people discontented. Most disaffected were merchants, artisans, workers, and peasants. The ideas of the Enlightenment thinkers brought new views of government and society. The American Revolution also influenced the coming of the French Revolution.

■ **Directions:** The following question is based on the accompanying documents in Part A. As you analyze the documents, take into account both the source of each document and the author's point of view. Be sure to do each of the following steps:

1. Carefully read the document-based question. Consider what you already know about this topic. How would you answer the question if you had no documents to examine?

2. Read each document carefully, underlining key phrases and words that address the document-based question. You may also wish to use the margin to make brief notes. Answer the questions that follow each document before moving on to the next document.

3. Based on your own knowledge and on the information found in the documents, formulate a thesis that directly answers the document-based question.

4. Organize supportive and relevant information into a brief outline.

5. Write a well-organized essay proving your thesis. You should present your essay logically. Include information both from the documents and from your own knowledge beyond the documents.

> **Question: What were the most important causes of the French Revolution? (Discuss three.)**

 PART A The following documents provide information about the French Revolution. Examine each document carefully. In the space provided, answer the question or questions that follow each document.

(continued)

DBQ 10: CAUSES OF THE FRENCH REVOLUTION

Document 1

In this adapted excerpt, Arthur Young describes his travels in France from 1787 to 1789.

> In the south of France there is a taille [tax on the land and its produce]. There is an injustice in levying the amount each person must pay. Lands held by the nobility are taxed very little. Lands held by commoners are taxed heavily. . . .
>
> September 5, 1788: The poor people seem very poor indeed. The children are terribly ragged.
>
> June 10, 1789: The lack of bread is terrible. Stories arrive every moment from the provinces of riots. . . . The price of bread has risen above people's ability to pay. This causes great misery.
>
> July 1789: . . . I was joined by a poor woman who complained of the hard times. "The tailles and feudal dues [rents owed the lords] are crushing us," she said.

Source: Arthur Young, *Travels in France and Italy During the Years 1787, 1788, and 1789*, E.P. Dutton & Co, 1927 (adapted)

What were three observations this traveler made about the life of peasants in France between 1787 and 1789?

_____

_____

_____

_____

_____

(continued)

DBQ 10: CAUSES OF THE FRENCH REVOLUTION

Document 2

This diagram illustrates the three French estates in 1789 and the land each held during the Old Regime.

FIRST ESTATE	SECOND ESTATE	THIRD ESTATE
Clergy	Nobles	
1% of the people owned 10% of the land	2% of the people owned 35% of the land	Middle class, peasants, city workers 97% of the people owned 55% of the land

What was the relationship between the percentage of the population in each estate and the percentage of land owned by that estate?

_____

_____

_____

Document 3

These are excerpts from the *cahiers* (lists of grievances about the king, taxing, and voting) brought to the Estates General.

> That the king be forced to reform the abuses and tyranny of lettre de cachet [a letter allowing a person to be jailed without trial].
>
> That every tax . . . be granted [by the Estates General] only for a limited time.
>
> That the taille [a tax on land] be borne equally by all classes. . . .
>
> The meetings of the Estates General . . . shall be scheduled for definite times. . . .
>
> In order to assure the third estate the influence it deserves because of its numbers, . . . its votes in the assembly should be taken and counted by head.

(continued)

DBQ 10: CAUSES OF THE FRENCH REVOLUTION

What changes in the French government did the third estate demand?

_____

_____

_____

_____

_____

Document 4

In *The French Revolution,* historian Albert Mathiez claimed that leadership fell to the middle class because of what those people knew about Enlightenment ideas.

> The Revolution had been accomplished in the minds of men long before it was translated into fact. . . .
>
> The middle class . . . was sensitive to their inferior legal position. The Revolution came from them—the middle class. The working classes were incapable of starting or controlling the Revolution. They were just beginning to learn to read.

Source: Albert Mathiez, *The French Revoluion,* Grosset & Dunlap, 1964 (adapted)

How did ideas impact the French Revolution, according to Mathiez? Why did the middle class, rather than the working class, drive the Revolution?

_____

_____

_____

_____

_____

(continued)

DBQ 10: CAUSES OF THE FRENCH REVOLUTION

Document 5

Lord Acton, a professor at Cambridge University, suggested another point of view.

> The condition of France alone did not bring about the overthrow of the monarchy. . . . For the sufferings of the people were not greater than they had been before. . . . The ideas of the philosophes were not directly responsible for the outbreak. . . .
>
> [T]he spark that changed thought into action was supplied by the Declaration of American Independence. . . . [T]he American example caused the Revolution to break out.

Source: Lord Acton, *Lectures on the French Revolution,* Macmillan, 1910 (adapted)

What did Lord Acton believe caused the French Revolution?

_____

_____

_____

_____

_____

 PART B   What were the most important causes of the French Revolution? (Discuss three.)

Grading Key

Document 1

Peasants had to pay high taxes and rents, while nobles were taxed lightly. The peasants were very poor; their children dressed in rags. Bread cost more than the peasants could afford to pay.

Document 2

Very few people occupied the first and second estates, yet they held 45 percent of the land. The third estate, which included by far the most people, held only 55 percent of the land.

Document 3

They wanted an end to the *lettre de cachet*; they wanted the Estates General to meet regularly; they wanted taxes to be limited and borne equally; they wanted their votes to be counted accurately.

Document 4

This author believed that the ideas of the Enlightenment had been in the minds of the people for a long time before action was taken. The middle class led the revolution because of their education and knowledge, which the working class lacked.

Document 5

Lord Acton believed that the examples of the American Revolution and the Declaration of Independence caused revolutionary ideas in France to be translated into action.

(continued)

DBQ 10: TEACHER PAGE

Additional Information Beyond the Documents

These documents provide students with only fragments of evidence. Essays should include relevant information beyond the documents—information that students have learned from their classroom study. The following list suggests some of the information from their outside learning that students might include in their essays.

- The ideas of Enlightenment writers—Locke, Rousseau, Voltaire

- Abuses of the Old Regime—incompetent absolute monarch Louis XVI

- Economic problems:

  - extravagant life at Versailles for the king and nobility

  - aid to the American Revolution

  - poor grain harvests

  - rigid class system and the opposition of the bourgeoisie

  - bankruptcy of the French government

  - calls for reform

Sample Student Essay

The French Revolution, which commenced in 1789, had a long list of causes. The most important long-range causes of this revolution, however, were the ideas of the Enlightenment, the unfair taxes, the gap between the rich and poor, and the American Revolution and Declaration of Independence.

The ideas of the Enlightenment influenced the French Revolution. The third estate, or the poorest social group, held very few rights socially or politically. But some of them, like doctors and lawyers, were educated and could read the new ideas of government from philosophers such as John Locke, Montesquieu, and Rousseau. "The Revolution had been accomplished in the minds of men long before it was translated into fact. . . ." (*Document 4*) These men spoke of democratic governments, with certain freedoms and natural rights. Eventually, the people of the third estate began to question their own government in France, and by the standards of these philosophers, demanded change. The cahiers (*Document 3*) reflect the ideas of the Enlightenment—democracy and equality.

As an economic cause, the unfair taxes also proved a cause for the French Revolution. Again, the third estate, composed of merchants, doctors, lawyers, and peasants, were taxed very heavily on many things: "In the south of France there is a taille [a tax on the land and its produce]" (*Document 1*). "Lands held by commoners

(continued)

are taxed heavily." Peasants also paid taxes to the clergy, nobles, and government. However, the richest estates, the clergy and nobles, paid little taxes or none at all despite their excess money, large land plots, and position and interaction with the government. "Lands held by the nobility are taxed very little." (*Document 1*) This unfair system angered the third estate, and prompted revolution.

As a social cause, in France there was a large gap between the rich and poor. A diagram (*Document 2*) shows this gap—there are very few members in the first and second estates, yet they owned the most land, while the third estate made up most of the population, yet owned very little land. In addition, as a political cause, the third estate had no privileges or say in the government, while both the clergy and nobles did. And as mentioned before, the inequality of taxes proved another gap in the social classes. These rules caused the formation of just upper and lower classes, no real middle. The third-estate population didn't have any way to move up in the social pyramid as a result of these restrictions. "The middle class [of the third estate] was sensitive to their inferior legal position. The Revolution came from them." (*Document 4*)

Finally, the influence of the American Revolution and the Declaration of Independence helped spur the French Revolution. Lord Acton (*Document 5*) stated, "The spark that changed thought into action was supplied by the Declaration of American Independence. . . . The American example caused the Revolution. . . ." By the colonists' influence, the French learned that if a small group of people could take on and defeat England, a very powerful country, they could do the same. The Americans helped encourage the Frenchmen's desire for freedom and democracy.

In conclusion, the French Revolution had its beginnings in many areas, but mostly in the inequalities felt by the common people, the new ideas of democracy and personal rights, and the examples of other revolutionists around them.

Teacher Comments

This essay addresses all aspects of the task. It identifies three major causes of the French Revolution. It includes outside information, details, and examples. It incorporates references to most of the documents. The essay is well organized and has a strong introduction and conclusion.

Score: 5

DBQ 11: ABSOLUTISM AND DEMOCRACY

Historical Context

People have used various forms of political systems throughout world history. Modern nation-states developed in Europe in the 1600s and 1700s. Absolute monarchs with vast power and wealth ruled countries such as France and Russia. At the same time in England, attempts were made to limit royal power and to protect the rights of some of the people. There was tension between absolutism and this limited form of democracy. Each of these systems of government had its advantages and disadvantages.

■ **Directions:** The following question is based on the accompanying documents in Part A. As you analyze the documents, take into account both the source of each document and the author's point of view. Be sure to do each of the following steps:

1. Carefully read the document-based question. Consider what you already know about this topic. How would you answer the question if you had no documents to examine?

2. Read each document carefully, underlining key phrases and words that address the document-based question. You may also wish to use the margin to make brief notes. Answer the questions that follow each document before moving on to the next document.

3. Based on your own knowledge and on the information found in the documents, formulate a thesis that directly answers the document-based question.

4. Organize supportive and relevant information into a brief outline.

5. Write a well-organized essay proving your thesis. You should present your essay logically. Include information both from the documents and from your own knowledge beyond the documents.

> **Question: What form of government was most effective—democracy or absolutism—for the seventeenth and eighteenth centuries in Europe?**

PART A The following documents relate to different types of government. Examine each document carefully. In the space provided, answer the questions that follow each document.

(continued)

DBQ 11: ABSOLUTISM AND DEMOCRACY

Document 1

This excerpt describes the characteristics of "men."

> For all men in general this observation may be made: they are ungrateful, fickle, and deceitful, eager to avoid dangers, and avid for gain, and while you are useful to them they are all with you, but when it [danger] approaches, they turn on you. Any prince, trusting only in their works and having no other preparations made, will fall to ruin, for friendships that are bought at a price and not by greatness and nobility of soul are paid for indeed, but they are not owned and cannot be called upon in time of need. Men have less hesitation in offending a man who is loved than one who is feared, for love is held by a bond of obligation which, as men are wicked, is broken whenever personal advantage suggests it, but fear is accompanied by the dread of punishment, which never relaxes.

Source: Niccolò Machiavelli, *The Prince*, 1513 (adapted)

According to Machiavelli, what type of ruler must the prince be? Why is it necessary for him to rule in this manner?

_____

_____

Document 2

These ideas were expressed by King James I of England in 1609.

> The state of monarchy is the supremest thing upon earth; for kings are not only God's lieutenants upon earth, and sit upon God's throne, but even by God Himself they are called gods. . . . Kings are justly called gods, for that they exercise a . . . divine power upon earth. . . . God hath power to create or destroy, make or unmake at His pleasure, to give life or send death, to judge all, and to be judged nor accountable to none; to raise low things, and to make high things low at His pleasure. . . . And the like power have kings.

What type of government does King James describe? Why does he believe it should be organized in this way?

_____

_____

_____

(continued)

DBQ 11: ABSOLUTISM AND DEMOCRACY

Document 3

These ideas were expressed by King Louis XIV of France in 1660.

> The head alone has the right to deliberate and decide, and the functions of all the other members consist only in carrying out the commands given to them. . . . The more you grant . . . [to the assembled people], the more it claims. . . . The interest of the state must come first.

What type of government does King Louis describe? Why does he recommend this type of government?

_____

_____

_____

_____

_____

Document 4

The following is an excerpt adapted from the writings of Voltaire. He was a French philosopher of the 1700s.

> I may disapprove of what you say, but I will defend to the death your right to say it. . . . The best government seems to be that in which all ranks of men are equally protected by the laws. . . .

What type of government does Voltaire recommend? What specific freedom does he feel is essential?

_____

_____

_____

_____

(continued)

DBQ 11: ABSOLUTISM AND DEMOCRACY

Document 5

In this excerpt, John Lock expresses his views on government.

> Men being . . . by nature all free, equal, and independent, no one can be . . . subjected to the political power of another without his own consent. . . . To protect natural rights governments are established. . . . Since men hope to preserve their property by establishing a government, they will not want that government to destroy their objectives. When legislators try to destroy or take away the property of the people, or try to reduce them to slavery, they put themselves into a state of war with the people who can then refuse to obey the laws.

Source: John Locke, *Two Treatises on Government,* 1690 (adapted)

Why is government established, according to Locke? What type of government does Locke describe? Under what circumstances can the people revolt?

_____

_____

_____

_____

_____

_____

Document 6

This excerpt provides another description of government.

> Although the forms of state—monarchy, aristocracy, and democracy—were united in English government, the powers of government were separated from one another. There can be no liberty where the executive, legislative, and judicial powers are united in one person or body of persons, because such concentration is bound to result in arbitrary despotism.

Source: Baron de Montesquieu, *The Spirit of the Laws,* 1748 (adapted)

(continued)

DBQ 11: ABSOLUTISM AND DEMOCRACY

What type of government does Montesquieu describe? Why does he believe it should be organized in this way?

_____

_____

_____

_____

_____

PART B

What form of government was most effective—democracy or absolutism—for the seventeenth and eighteenth centuries in Europe?

Grading Key

Document 1

Because people are untrustworthy and "wicked," the ruler must instill fear in his subjects. They must fear him rather than love him if he wants to maintain control.

Document 2

King James describes absolute monarchy. James believes in the "divine right" of kings. Consequently, he feels that the king is God's lieutenant and sits in His place on earth. Kings have "like power" to God. They have the power to do anything they need or desire to do. There are no limitations on their power.

Document 3

King Louis describes absolute monarchy. He says that the interests of the state are more important than those of the individual. The king, as head of the government, must give the orders, and the subjects must carry them out as directed. The king must govern in this manner because it is in the best interests of the state. In addition, the people will continue to ask for more if given any voice.

Document 4

Voltaire says that the best government is one that protects all people equally—a democracy. He believes that freedom of speech is essential.

Document 5

According to Locke, governments are established to protect the natural rights of men. Governments derive their power from the governed, who give their consent. Consequently, the people have established a democratic government. Under specific conditions, such as when the government tries to assume more power at the expense of the people, the people have the right to revolt and take back the power they have given to the government.

Document 6

Montesquieu describes a division of power in a basically democratic government. He stresses the importance of dividing the power so that no one branch or person has all the power, thus preventing despotism.

(continued)

Additional Information Beyond the Documents

These documents provide students with only fragments of evidence. Essays should include relevant information beyond the documents—information that students have learned from their classroom study. The following list suggests some of the information from their outside learning that students might include in their essays.

- Positive and negative characteristics of the rule of monarchs such as Louis XIV in France, Peter the Great in Russia, Philip II in Spain, and Elizabeth I and James I in England

- Understanding of political systems of absolutism and democracy, natural rights, and other ideas of the Enlightenment writers such as Montesquieu and Voltaire

Sample Student Essay

Absolutism, which put unlimited power in the hands of the monarch, and democracy, which placed power in the hands of the people, have been important forms of government through history. Yet absolutism, in my opinion, proved to be the most effective form of government in the seventeenth and eighteenth centuries. This is supported by well-known absolute monarchs King James I and King Louis XIV of France, as well as Machiavelli in *The Prince*. For the time period, absolutism was the most efficient government as decisions were made quickly so that the people had their needs met. In addition, at that time divine right rule was accepted by most people. But in the future the ideas of democracy would take hold.

First, absolute monarchies are efficient. In an absolute monarchy, there is one head, not whole groups of people to converse with about a new law or idea; therefore decisions are made quickly, and with the benefit of the state in mind. "The head alone has the right to deliberate and decide, and the functions of all the other members consist only in carrying out the commands given to them. . . . The interest of the state must come first" (*Document 3*). Here King Louis of France described the positive aspects of an absolute monarch. In contrast, Montesquieu suggested that executive, legislative, and judicial powers share power. (*Document 6*) But this democratic government took too much time—the decision had to go through many people. In the seventeenth and eighteenth centuries, government could not survive the time required, but in the future centuries it would.

In addition, the absolute monarch was positive for its time period in the sense that absolute monarchs provided the people with what they needed, like roads and other public buildings and developed manufacturing. King Louis describes this through: "The interest of the state must come first." The decisions made by the absolute monarch clearly reflect a beneficial result for the people. However, in the future, a one-person decision would fail to meet the needs of the people as not only

(continued)

would people want a say in their government, but also wanted ". . . [to be] by nature all free, equal and independent, no one can be . . . subjected to the political power of another without his own consent" (*Document 5*).

Finally, absolute monarchs of the seventeenth and eighteenth centuries claimed their power was supreme, ". . . for kings are not only God's lieutenants . . . but even by God himself they are called gods" (*Document 2*). By providing a reason for power, the people could easily be assured that the power of their ruler was genuine and they accepted it. However, this "divine right" theory created a fear among the people of the king, a positive aspect in Machiavelli's view: "Men have less hesitation in offending a man who is loved than one who is feared . . . fear is accompanied by the dread of punishment, which never relaxes" (*Document 1*). The people obeyed. However, once again, this theory would prove negative in the future, as new thinking emerged; in the writings of Voltaire, ". . . I will defend your right to say it [your opinion]" (*Document 4*). This statement defends the freedom of speech—something that the people living in the early times of monarchies knew nothing about.

In conclusion, absolutism proved an effective way of government for the seventeenth and eighteenth centuries. It provided a sense of stability, created order, and then, in the future, with new age thinkers and ideas, the old ways of the absolute monarchies would fail to survive.

Teacher Comments

This student essay takes a position and supports it with evidence—providing three reasons why absolutism was the most efficient form of government for the seventeenth and eighteenth centuries. The student both incorporates the documents and includes outside information. Structurally, the essay is well organized, with an introduction and conclusion. The essay lacks clarity due to the references to the future, when the ideas of the Enlightenment and democracy will be implemented.

Score: 4

Name _____   Date _____

DBQ 12: THE INDUSTRIAL REVOLUTION: BEGINNINGS

Historical Context

The Industrial Revolution was a rapid, greatly increased output of machine-made goods. It began in England in the 1700s within the textile industry. Before the Industrial Revolution, people wove textiles by hand at home. Beginning in the mid-1700s, machines did this and other jobs as well. At the same time, greatly improved farming methods resulted in an agricultural revolution. This paved the way for changes in manufacturing techniques. In the 1800s, the Industrial Revolution spread from England to continental Europe and North America.

■ **Directions:** The following question is based on the accompanying documents in Part A. As you analyze the documents, take into account both the source of each document and the author's point of view. Be sure to do each of the following steps:

1. Carefully read the document-based question. Consider what you already know about this topic. How would you answer the question if you had no documents to examine?

2. Read each document carefully, underlining key phrases and words that address the document-based question. You may also wish to use the margin to make brief notes. Answer the questions that follow each document before moving on to the next document.

3. Based on your own knowledge and on the information found in the documents, formulate a thesis that directly answers the document-based question.

4. Organize supportive and relevant information into a brief outline.

5. Write a well-organized essay proving your thesis. You should present your essay logically. Include information both from the documents and from your own knowledge beyond the documents.

Question: Why did the Industrial Revolution begin in England?

PART A
The following documents discuss aspects of the Industrial Revolution. Examine each document carefully. In the space provided, answer the question or questions that follow each document.

(continued)

DBQ 12: THE INDUSTRIAL REVOLUTION: BEGINNINGS

Document 1

This map shows the resources and canals of England in the eighteenth century.

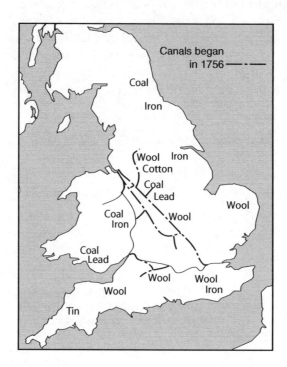

According to the map, what resources did England have that were needed for industrialization?

_____

_____

Document 2

This excerpt is from a testimony presented before England's Factory Commission in 1833.

> You have been a witness of the operative [working] class in these parts; you have seen it grow from nothing into a great body in the space of a few years: how was it recruited? . . . A good many from the agricultural parts. . . . People left other occupations and came to spinning for the sake of the high wages.

(continued)

DBQ 12: THE INDUSTRIAL REVOLUTION: BEGINNINGS

Why were workers readily available for factory jobs? _____

_____

_____

Document 3

This excerpt describes the assembly line used in factories during the eighteenth century.

> I have seen a small manufactory [factory] of this kind where ten men only were employed, and where some of them performed two or three distinct operations. . . . They could . . . make among them . . . upwards of 48,000 pins in a day. . . . But if they had all wrought [worked] separately and independently . . . they certainly could not each of them have made twenty . . . in a day.

Source: Adam Smith, *Wealth of Nations*, 1776 (adapted)

According to Smith, why were workers in a factory so productive? _____

_____

_____

Document 4

This excerpt describes the industrialization of England.

> England . . . has been fortunate in possessing the natural conditions necessary to success. . . . We recognize that England is rich in these advantages, that she has coal and iron lying close together, that her sheep give the best wool, that her harbors are plentiful, that she is not ill-off for rivers, and that no part of the country is farther than seventy miles from the sea.

Source: George Warner, *Landmarks in English Industrial History*, Blackie and Son, 1899 (adapted)

How did geography help England industrialize? _____

_____

_____

(continued)

DBQ 12: THE INDUSTRIAL REVOLUTION: BEGINNINGS

Document 5

This excerpt comments on innovations during the Industrial Revolution.

> Systematic thought lay behind most of the innovations in industrial practice. Invention . . . rarely thrives in a community of simple peasants or unskilled manual laborers: only when division of labor has developed . . . does it come to harvest. The stream of English scientific thought was one of the main tributaries [causes] of the industrial revolution . . . discoveries in different fields of activity were linked together. . . .

Source: Thomas S. Ashton, *The Industrial Revolution*, Oxford University Press, 1962 (adapted)

How did innovation lead to the Industrial Revolution in England?

_____

_____

Document 6

The following chart identifies important inventions during the eighteenth century.

Changes in Textile Machinery

Inventor	Invention	Importance
John Kay	flying shuttle	increased speed of weaving
James Hargreaves	spinning jenny	spun 8–10 threads at a time; used at home
Richard Arkwright	water frame	large spinning machine in factory, driven by water
Edmund Cartwright	power loom	water powered; automatically wove thread into cloth
Eli Whitney	cotton gin	separated seed from raw cotton

Which three inventions were most important in increasing textile production? Explain.

_____

_____

_____

_____

(continued)

DBQ 12: THE INDUSTRIAL REVOLUTION: BEGINNINGS

Document 7

This chart identifies agricultural changes during the Industrial Revolution.

Changes in Agriculture

Inventor	Invention	Importance
Jethro Tull	horse-drawn seen drill	planted seeds in straight rows
Robtert Blakewell	stock breeding	improved quality of animals to produce more meat, milk, and wool
Cyrus McCormick	mechanical reaper	made grain harvesting easier

What was the result of these changes in agriculture in England?

_____

_____

_____

_____

_____

Document 8

This excerpt comments on farming methods in England.

> As I shall leave Norfolk, it is proper to give a review of the farming methods which have made . . . this country so famous in the farming world. . . . The great improvements have been made by the following methods.
>
> - By enclosing without the help of Parliament
>
> - By the introduction of a four year rotation of crops
>
> - By growing turnips, clover, and rye grass
>
> - By the country being divided chiefly into large farms

Source: Arthur Young, *A Farmer's Tour Through the East of England*, 1771 (adapted)

(continued)

DBQ 12: THE INDUSTRIAL REVOLUTION: BEGINNINGS

How did these four changes in agriculture enable England to industrialize more easily?

_____

_____

_____

_____

_____

Document 9

This excerpt describes English industrialization.

> When one realizes the thousands of internal tariffs that obstructed [slowed down] traffic in Germany up to 1834 and the innumerable tolls and charges that hindered trade in France before 1789 . . . it is clear that the political and economic freedom in England was one of the causes of her industrial expansion.

Source: L.C.A. Knowles, *The Industrial and Commercial Revolutions in Great Britain During the Nineteenth Century*, E.P. Dutton & Co., 1921 (adapted)

What are two reasons Knowles cited to explain industrialization in England?

_____

_____

_____

_____

PART B Why did the Industrial Revolution begin in England?

Grading Key

Document 1

The resources included coal, iron, lead, tin, and wool. Canals connected the rivers to the seacoast so that products could be transported easily.

Document 2

This excerpt indicates that many workers were available for the factories. Workers came from rural areas, since fewer workers were needed there. They also came to the cities because they wanted the "high wages."

Document 3

The men were so productive because of specialization of labor. Each man performed several specific tasks. This was more productive than if the men worked separately.

Document 4

England had the resources and conditions needed for industrialization: coal and iron; sheep with the best wool; many harbors, rivers, and seaports.

Document 5

England had people with technical and scientific knowledge. They were able to make the necessary inventions and discoveries.

Document 6

All these inventions increased textile production. Students choose and explain three of these advances. The flying shuttle increased the speed of weaving. The spinning jenny allowed spinners to keep up with the new, speedy weaving devices. The power loom automatically wove thread into cloth. The water frame drove spinning wheels with water power rather than by hand. The cotton gin separated seeds from raw cotton quickly.

(continued)

Document 7

The drill and the reaper made it possible to increase food production and decrease the number of farmers needed to produce the food. Consequently, there were more workers available for factory jobs. Stock breeding advances also produced more food, and also more wool for the textile factories.

Document 8

Enclosure created large farms and displaced small farmers, who became part of the worker pool for the factories. Larger farms, crop rotation, and the planting of crops that replenished nutrients in the soil moved farming from self-sufficiency to large outputs capable of sustaining the growing population of factory workers.

Document 9

England had no internal tariffs, tolls, and charges to block trade. England's political and economic freedom allowed industrial expansion to occur unhindered.

Additional Information Beyond the Documents

The documents provide students with only fragments of evidence. Answers should include relevant information beyond the documents—information that students have learned from their classroom study. The following list suggests some of the information from outside learning that students might include in their essays.

- Reasons why industrialization began in England: natural resources, capital, markets, workers, positive governmental policies, transportation, power sources

- Agricultural revolution—Enclosure Acts

- Inventions/technology

DBQ 13: NATIONALISM IN THE NINETEENTH CENTURY

Historical Context

Nationalism was the most powerful force in the 1800s. It came to the fore with the French Revolution of 1789. It then contributed to the unification of Italy and Germany in the nineteenth century. At the same time, ethnic unrest threatened to topple the Ottoman and the Austro-Hungarian empires. Nationalism also contributed to the outbreak of wars. These included the Franco-Prussian War and World War I.

■ **Directions:** The following question is based on the accompanying documents in Part A. As you analyze the documents, take into account both the source of each document and the author's point of view. Be sure to do each of the following steps:

1. Carefully read the document-based question. Consider what you already know about this topic. How would you answer the question if you had no documents to examine?

2. Read each document carefully, underlining key phrases and words that address the document-based question. You may also wish to use the margin to make brief notes. Answer the questions that follow each document before moving on to the next document.

3. Based on your own knowledge and on the information found in the documents, formulate a thesis that directly answers the document-based question.

4. Organize supportive and relevant information into a brief outline.

5. Write a well-organized essay proving your thesis. You should present your essay logically. Include information both from the documents and from your own knowledge beyond the documents.

> **Question: How would you evaluate the following statements?**
> **Nationalism united people into nation-states.**
> **It toppled empires composed of many ethnic minorities.**
> **It contributed to the outbreak of wars in the nineteenth century.**

PART A   The following documents provide information about nationalism as a force in nineteenth-century Europe. Examine each document carefully. In the space provided, answer the question or questions that follow each document.

(continued)

DBQ 13: NATIONALISM IN THE NINETEENTH CENTURY

Document 1

This excerpt describes the *Levée en Masse.*

> The young men will go forth to battle; the married men will make arms and transport food; the women will make tents and uniforms and will serve in the hospitals; the children will prepare lint from old linens; the old people will gather in public places to raise the courage of the warriors, to excite hatred of kings, and to preach the unity of the Republic.

Source: French Committee of Public Safety, *Levée en Masse*, 1793 (adapted)

What impact did the *Levée en Masse* have on the French people? _____

_____

_____

Document 2

"La Marseillaise," the French national anthem, aroused the emotions of the French people during the revolution.

> Arise, children of the fatherland,
> Our day of glory has arrived.
> Against us cruel tyrants
> Have raised their bloody flag.
> Do you hear in the countryside
> Their fierce hired soldiers?
> They come almost into your arms
> To attack your children and your fields.
>
> *Chorus:*
> To arms, citizens!
> Form your battalions!
> March on, march on,
> To liberty or death!

What did the national anthem urge the French to do? _____

_____

_____

_____

(continued)

Name _____   Date _____

DBQ 13: NATIONALISM IN THE NINETEENTH CENTURY

Document 3

This excerpt is from Count Cavour, who was named prime minister of Piedmont-Sardinia in 1852. As a diplomat, he provided the "brains" of Italian unification.

> We ardently wish to free Italy from foreign rule. . . . We want to drive out the foreigners not only because we want to see our country powerful and glorious, but because we want to elevate the Italian people in intelligence and moral development.

What action did Cavour recommend in this excerpt?

_____

_____

_____

Document 4

Giuseppe Garibaldi was the "sword" of Italian unification. He added the southern Kingdom of the Two Sicilies to Italy in 1860. He described his soldiers, known as Red Shirts, with these words.

> O noble Thousand! . . . I love to remember you! . . . Where any of our brothers are fighting for liberty, there all Italians must hasten!—such was your motto. Let him who loves his country in his heart, and not with his lips only, follow me.

What was Garibaldi trying to accomplish in this speech?

_____

_____

_____

(continued)

103   *Document-Based Assessment for Global History*

DBQ 13: NATIONALISM IN THE NINETEENTH CENTURY

Document 5

These words were spoken by Otto von Bismarck, prime minister of Prussia, in 1866. Some people feel that Bismarck single-handedly unified Germany and started it on its road to greatness. Here, Bismarck explained the process for unification of Germany.

> I had shown plainly the direction in which I was going. Prussia . . . could no longer carry alone the power that Germany required for its security. That must be equally distributed over all German peoples. We would get not nearer our goal by speeches, associations, or decisions by the majority. We would not be able to avoid serious contest with Austria. This contest could only be settled by blood and iron. There is one way to guarantee our success. The deputies must place the greatest possible weight of blood and iron in the hands of the King of Prussia.

What was Bismarck's method for uniting Germany?

_____

_____

_____

Document 6

This excerpt is adapted from a testimony given by Gavrilo Princip at his trial for the 1914 assassination of Archduke Franz Ferdinand.

> . . . I am a nationalist. I aimed to free the Yugoslavs. For I am a Yugoslav. . . . As far as Serbia is concerned, it is her duty to free us.

Who does Princip say he is, and what is he doing?

_____

_____

_____

(continued)

DBQ 13: NATIONALISM IN THE NINETEENTH CENTURY

Document 7

This illustration shows the effect of nationalism among the subject nationalities of the Austro-Hungarian Empire.

Based on this illustration, what was the effect of nationalism on the Austrian Empire?

_____

_____

_____

PART B

How would you evaluate the following statements?
Nationalism united people into nation-states.
It toppled empires composed of many ethnic minorities.
It contributed to the outbreak of wars in the nineteenth century.

Grading Key

Document 1

Everyone had a role to play as the French united to fight against the other European countries that were attacking France.

Document 2

This national anthem urged the people to unite for the fatherland against the cruel tyrants and their mercenary soldiers. The French must take up arms and march together for "liberty or death." This was an emotional call to action and unity.

Document 3

Cavour believed the Italians must end control by foreign countries, like Austria, in order to unite Italy.

Document 4

Garibaldi expressed the importance of military action as he motivated his Red Shirts to fight for liberty out of love for their country.

Document 5

Bismarck, a nationalist, said that Prussia needed the support of all Germans in the unification movement. Furthermore, they must unite behind the king of Prussia to wage war—"blood and iron"—against Austria.

Document 6

Princip says he is a nationalist and a Yugoslav, fighting to free and unite his Yugoslav people.

Document 7

The illustration shows that nationalism was blowing apart the Austrian Empire because its subject nationalities wanted their own countries.

(continued)

DBQ 13: TEACHER PAGE

Additional Information Beyond the Documents

These documents provide students with only fragments of evidence. Essays should include relevant information beyond the documents—information that students have learned from their classroom study. The following list suggests some of the information from outside learning that students might include in their essays.

- Nationalist leaders, their methods, and events that resulted in the unification of Germany and Italy

- The Austrian and Ottoman empires and the demands of their ethnic groups for independence (for example, Yugoslavia in modern times)

- Wars caused by nationalism—including World War I, World War II, and the Franco-Prussian War

Sample Student Essay

Nationalism, which began in the 1700s through the events of the French Revolution, became a powerful force in Europe in the later nineteenth century. As it grew, nationalism united people in [the] countries of Germany and Italy. Yet it also divided the Ottoman and Austro-Hungarian empires and led to the outbreak of wars.

Unification occurred as a result of nationalism, which developed between groups of people of similar culture, religion, language, and traditions. During the French Revolution nationalism was evident in the Levée en Masse ". . . young men will go forth to battle . . . women will make tents . . . old people will gather in public places to raise the courage of the warriors . . ." (*Document 1*) to fight a common enemy for common goals. The French national anthem (*Document 2*) also encouraged them to fight together. A similar feeling spread to Germany and Italy. In Germany, nationalism was encouraged by Otto von Bismarck, nicknamed the "iron chancellor." He believed that uniting Germany had to occur with ". . . blood and iron . . ." (*Document 5*). Bismarck disliked passive ways of decision making like speeches or voting; rather he wanted to fight, and provoke war, as he did with Austria in the Seven Weeks War, and France in the Franco-Prussian War. With blood and iron he united Germany, either by winning the land in war or through creating nationalism, which joined independent states to form the whole country. In Italy, prime minister Count Cavour, who provided the brains and acted as diplomat of Italian unification, stated, "We . . . wish to free Italy from foreign rule. We want to drive out the foreigners . . . because we want to elevate the Italian people in intelligence and moral development" (*Document 3*). Because of the separate Italian states and its partial rule by the Austrian Empire, the Italians were very much separated. Yet, as nationalism grew, the Italian people came together as a whole to

(continued)

free the areas in the north and south from foreign rule. Giuseppe Garibaldi, the "sword" of unification, helped bring southern Italy to complete unification with his Red Shirts. He said, "Where any of our brothers are fighting for liberty, there all Italians must hasten!" (*Document 4*). Nationalism grew, so that like Germany, the states came together as the whole country of Italy.

However, nationalism also caused disunification, by creating wars and breaking up empires. As in the Austro-Hungarian Empire, there were many different ethnic groups, as shown in an illustration in Document 7. Nationalism separated these people, and they soon demanded to be separate nation-states. The Austrian Empire declined as the Hungarians, who made up a majority of the empire, demanded a say in government; the empire was then called the Austro-Hungarian Empire. Soon the other groups in the empire developed nationalism and wanted their own countries. "I am a nationalist. I aimed to free the Yugoslavs. For I am a Yugoslav. . . ," said a Serb. (*Document 6*) World War I brought the end of this once powerful Austrian Empire. A similar situation occurred within the Ottoman Empire. After Suleiman the Great died, a line of very weak sultans followed, which weakened the empire as nationalism grew among the mixed ethnic groups, leading to the Balkan War. The Ottomans were too weak to maintain order. Revolution, beginning with the Greeks' war for independence in 1830, was followed by other ethnic unrest so that by the end of World War I, the Ottoman Empire had been destroyed.

However, wars also resulted from nationalism. Wars not only ended in disunification, as the Balkan War weakened the Ottoman Empire, but they also were used in unification—von Bismarck's Seven Weeks War and the Franco-Prussian War brought together the German states. Also, the Italians fought their way to unification of the northern and southern foreign-dominated areas through wars.

In conclusion, nationalism was a driving force in both the unification and disunification of countries and empires in Europe. Nationalism can obviously be assumed to be one of the most powerful movements in history, for it helped in creating the countries and cultures that we know or even descend from today.

Teacher Comments

This essay addresses all aspects of the task. It describes how nationalism united Italy and Germany, as well as divided the Ottoman and Austro-Hungarian empires with wars. It integrates outside information with information from the documents. The essay is well organized and has a strong introduction and conclusion.

Score: 5

DBQ 14: JAPAN'S MODERNIZATION

Historical Context

In the early 1600s, Japan had closed itself to almost all contacts with the outside world. In the mid-1800s, Japan was faced with a challenge to its policy of isolation. As a result, Japan started to modernize. It emerged in the twentieth century as a major world power.

■ **Directions:** The following question is based on the accompanying documents in Part A. As you analyze the documents, take into account both the source of each document and the author's point of view. Be sure to do each of the following steps:

1. Carefully read the document-based question. Consider what you already know about this topic. How would you answer the question if you had no documents to examine?

2. Read each document carefully, underlining key phrases and words that address the document-based question. You may also wish to use the margin to make brief notes. Answer the questions that follow each document before moving on to the next document.

3. Based on your own knowledge and on the information found in the documents, formulate a thesis that directly answers the document-based question.

4. Organize supportive and relevant information into a brief outline.

5. Write a well-organized essay proving your thesis. You should present your essay logically. Include information both from the documents and from your own knowledge beyond the documents.

Question: How did Japan emerge as a world power, going from isolation to modernization to imperialism? What were the results—positive and negative—of Japan's modernization?

The following documents deal with developments in Japan from the 1600s to the 1900s. Examine each document carefully. In the space provided, answer the question or questions that follow each document.

(continued)

DBQ 14: JAPAN'S MODERNIZATION

Document 1

The following time line outlines important dates in Japan's history.

> 1603—Tokugawa shogunate begins.
>
> 1635—Closed Country Edict cuts Japan off from rest of world.
>
> 1639—Portuguese are expelled; Dutch and Chinese are permitted to trade at Nagasaki.
>
> 1853–54—U.S. Commodore Perry visits Japan.
>
> 1867—Meiji Restoration; the emperor takes over power.
>
> 1889—Meiji Constitution is adopted.
>
> 1894–95—Sino-Japanese War; Japan gains Taiwan and domination of Korea.
>
> 1904–05—Russo-Japanese War; Japan acquires Port Arthur and Russia's position in Manchuria.
>
> 1910—Japan annexes Korea.
>
> 1931—Japan invades Manchuria and sets up a puppet state.
>
> 1937—Japan invades China.
>
> 1940—"Greater East Asia Co-Prosperity Sphere" plan is recommended.
>
> 1941—Japan attacks Pearl Harbor and sets out to conqueror the Pacific region.
>
> 1945—End of World War II; Japan surrenders.

Write two events from the list above under each heading below.

Relative Isolation

1.

2.

Modernization

1.

2.

Imperialism

1.

2.

(continued)

DBQ 14: JAPAN'S MODERNIZATION

Document 2

This excerpt is adapted from Japan's Closed Country Edict of 1635.

> Japanese ships may absolutely not leave for foreign countries.
>
> No Japanese person is allowed to go abroad. Anyone who tries to do so will be put to death.
>
> All Japanese persons who live abroad will be put to death when they return home. . . . Samurai [paid warriors] may not purchase goods from foreign ships directly from foreign merchants in Nagasaki.

What policy did the Closed Country Edict establish? _____

_____

How did this edict affect Japanese traders?

_____

_____

Document 3

This excerpt is adapted from a letter sent by U.S. Commodore Perry to the Emperor of Japan on July 7, 1853.

> The government of the United States desires to obtain from . . . Japan some positive assurances that persons who may be shipwrecked on the coast of Japan, or driven by stress of weather into her ports, shall be treated with humanity. . . . Therefore, as the United States and Japan are becoming every day nearer and nearer to each other, the President desires to live in peace and friendship with your imperial majesty, but no friendship can long exist, unless Japan ceases to act toward Americans as if they were her enemies. . . .
>
> Many of the large ships-of-war destined to visit Japan have not yet arrived in these seas, though they are hourly expected; and the undersigned, as an evidence of his friendly intentions, has brought but four of the smaller ones, designing, should it become necessary, to return to Yedo [Tokyo] in the ensuing spring with a much larger force. . . .
>
> M.C. Perry

(continued)

DBQ 14: JAPAN'S MODERNIZATION

What reason did Perry give for his visit to Japan?

_____

_____

_____

Document 4

The following excerpts are adapted from an agreement signed between the United States and Japan on March 31, 1854.

> The United States of America and the Empire of Japan . . . have resolved to fix . . . the rules which shall in future be mutually observed. . . .
>
> Article II. The port[s] of Simoda and of Hakodade . . . are granted by the Japanese as ports for the reception of American ships, where they can be supplied with wood, water, provisions, and coal. . . .
>
> Article III. Whenever ships of the United States are thrown or wrecked on the coast of Japan, the Japanese vessels will assist them. . . .
>
> Article VII. It is agreed that ships of the United States . . . [in] the ports open to them shall be permitted to [trade]. . .

What was Japan giving to the United States in this agreement?

_____

_____

_____

Was this evidence of a lessening of Japanese isolation? Explain.

_____

_____

_____

(continued)

DBQ 14: JAPAN'S MODERNIZATION

Document 5

A temporary constitution giving power to the emperor had been adopted in 1868. This ended the power of the Tokugawa shogun. The Meiji Constitution of 1889 was regarded as the permanent constitution of Japan. Here are some excerpts from it.

> Article I. The Empire of Japan shall be reigned over and governed by a line of Emperors unbroken for ages eternal.
>
> Article III. The Emperor is sacred and inviolable.
>
> Article XI. The Emperor has supreme command of the Army and Navy.
>
> Article XLV. When the House of Representatives has been ordered to dissolve, Members shall be caused by Imperial Order to be newly elected.

Source: Alfred Stead, editor, *Japan by the Japanese,* William Heinemann, 1904 (adapted)

How did this governmental structure strengthen the central government?

_____

_____

_____

Document 6

This excerpt, attained from the full powers given to Lord Iwakura and the other ambassadors, describes the mission of a group sent to Europe and the United States by the Japanese emperor in 1871.

> The time for the revision of the existing treaties will arrive in less than a year, and we wish to revise them considerably so as to place Japan on the footing of equality with the civilized nations. . . . We do not intend to undertake the revision at once. We will first study the institutions of the civilized nations, adopt those most suited to Japan, and gradually reform our government and manners, so as to attain the status equal to that of the civilized nations.

Source: Alfred Stead, editor, *Japan by the Japanese,* William Heinemann, 1904 (adapted)

(continued)

DBQ 14: JAPAN'S MODERNIZATION

What did the emperor plan to do, and why?

_____

_____

_____

_____

_____

Document 7

In this excerpt, Baron Kentaro Kaneko, the Japanese minister of commerce and agriculture, expressed his opinion for modernization.

> Japan . . . occupies a small amount of land and has a large population, with little material out of which to manufacture, hence has to rely upon the material imported from other countries. We have coal, but not sufficient iron, and almost no gold. Hence, in my opinion, Japan must stand as an industrial country. . . . An agricultural policy is not bad. It was satisfactory in the feudal period—that is, for so long as we were not pressed by the Russians, [the] English, and the Americans from all sides. But the conditions are otherwise today. The Pacific is becoming the center of the struggle in which we are called to compete with much stronger foes. Japan as an agricultural country cannot stand against Russia, Australia, Canada, or America. Hence we must try other means for the struggle—that is, we must obtain raw materials from them and manufacture them for the Asiatic markets.

Source: Alfred Stead, editor, *Japan by the Japanese,* William Heinemann, 1904 (adapted)

What economic changes did the Japanese minister recommend, and why?

_____

_____

_____

How would Japan get the materials it needed?

_____

_____

(continued)

DBQ 14: JAPAN'S MODERNIZATION

Document 8

This graph illustrates imports and exports in Japan during the Meiji Rule from 1868 to 1912.

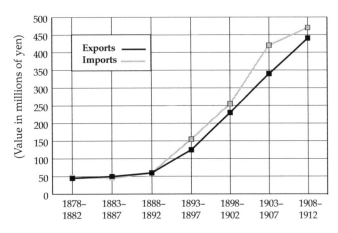

Source: New York Regents Exam, 2002 (adapted)

According to this graph, what economic change occurred during the period of Meiji rule?

_____

_____

Document 9

Japan declared war on Russia on February 10, 1904. This is an excerpt from Japan's declaration.

> We hereby declare war against Russia. . . . The integrity of Korea is a matter of constant concern to this Empire, not only because of our traditional relations with that country, but because the separate existence of Korea is essential to the safety of our realm. Nevertheless Russia . . . is still in occupation of Manchuria, has consolidated and strengthened her hold upon those provinces, and is bent upon their final annexation. . . [T]he safety of Korea is in danger; the vital interests of our Empire are menaced. The guarantees for the future which we have failed to secure by peaceful negotiations we can now only seek by our appeal to arms.

Source: Alfred Stead, editor, *Japan by the Japanese,* William Heinemann, 1904 (adapted)

(continued)

DBQ 14: JAPAN'S MODERNIZATION

What reasons did Japan give for declaring war on Russia?

_____

_____

Document 10

This map details the valuable natural resources found in Korea and Manchuria in 1934.

Source: Elisabeth Gaynor Ellis and Anthony Esler, *World History Connections to Today: The Modern Era*, Prentice Hall, 2002 (adapted)

Based on the map, why would Japan want to acquire Korea and Manchuria?

_____

_____

_____

(continued)

DBQ 14: JAPAN'S MODERNIZATION

Document 11

In 1940, the Japanese Total War Research Institute produced the following plan for the establishment of a "Greater East Asia Co-Prosperity Sphere."

> The Japanese empire is a manifestation of morality, and its special characteristic is the propagation of the Imperial Way. . . . It is necessary . . . to cause East Asia to return to its original form of independence and co-prosperity by shaking off the yoke of Europe and America. . . . In the Union of East Asia, the Japanese empire is at once the stabilizing power and the leading influence. . . . [A basic step will be] the construction of a new China in tune with the rapid construction of the Inner Sphere. Aggressive American and British influences in East Asia shall be driven out of the area of Indo-China and the South Seas, and this area shall be brought into our defense sphere. The war with Britain and America shall be prosecuted for that purpose. . . . [T]he Japanese empire is the center . . . of Oriental moral and cultural reconstruction.

According to this document, what was the ultimate goal of the Japanese empire?

_____

_____

_____

_____

 PART B How did Japan emerge as a world power, going from isolation to modernization to imperialism? What were the results—positive and negative—of Japan's modernization?

DBQ 14: TEACHER PAGE

Grading Key

Document 1

Students should write two events under each heading.

Relative Isolation

1. Closed Country Edict cuts Japan off.

2. Portuguese are expelled.

Modernization

1. Meiji Restoration—the emperor takes power.

2. Meiji Constitution is adopted.

Imperialism

1. Japan annexes Korea.

2. Japan invades Manchuria.

3. Japan invades China.

4. "Greater East Asia Co-Prosperity Sphere" plan is recommended.

5. Japan attacks Pearl Harbor and sets out to conquer the Pacific region.

Document 2

It established Japanese isolation. Japanese traders were not allowed out of the country. Trade was very limited.

Document 3

Perry wrote that he visited Japan to get an agreement by the Japanese government to assist persons who were shipwrecked on the coast of Japan.

Document 4

Japan was opening two ports to resupply American ships with wood, water, provisions, and coal. Japan was also agreeing to provide assistance for the shipwrecked. This was what the United States hoped to gain by Perry's visit; it was a breach of Japan's policy of isolation.

(continued)

Document 5

The Constitution of 1889 provided a strong emperor who would be able to control the central government so the country would be more unified.

Document 6

The emperor was sending people to the "civilized," or industrialized, countries to gather information on how each one organized its economy and military. He was doing this so that Japan could modernize by adopting the institutions that were suited for Japan. The emperor wanted the "civilized nations" to treat Japan as an equal.

Document 7

The minister recommended that Japan become an industrialized nation so that it could compete with others for control in the Pacific region and for the Asian markets. Japan would have to buy raw materials from other nations.

Document 8

Under the Meiji, Japan greatly increased its imports and exports as it industrialized.

Document 9

Japan declared war on Russia to protect Korea and to prevent Russian annexation of Manchuria.

Document 10

Japan might want Korea and Manchuria because they had deposits of coal, petroleum, gold, iron ore, and bauxite.

Document 11

Japan wanted to rid East Asia of European and American influence, and to establish the Japanese empire as the center of an Asian sphere.

(continued)

DBQ 14: TEACHER PAGE

Additional Information Beyond the Documents

These documents provide students with only fragments of evidence. Essays should include relevant information beyond the documents—information that students have learned from their classroom study, outside reading and viewing, and other learning experiences. The following list suggests some of that information.

- Japanese history in the seventeenth through twentieth centuries, including the following:

    - knowledge of the period of isolation

    - knowledge of the modernization under the Meiji

    - knowledge of the expansion of Japan in the twentieth century

Additional Activities

The following may be offered to students as additional activities:

- Evaluate Japan's emergence as a world power in the 1940s.

- Develop a DBQ essay that compares industrialization in Japan and England by choosing specific documents from this DBQ and from DBQ 12 about the Industrial Revolution.

DBQ 15: NEW IMPERIALISM: CAUSES

Historical Context

Between 1870 and 1920, the rate of European imperialism increased. This was due to economic, political, and social forces. The Industrial Revolution stirred the ambitions of European nations. The advances in technology allowed these nations to spread their control over the less-developed areas of the world. Historians have studied this empire-building frenzy. They have offered a variety of perspectives on its causes.

■ **Directions:** The following question is based on the accompanying documents in Part A. As you analyze the documents, take into account both the source of each document and the author's point of view. Be sure to do each of the following steps:

1. Carefully read the document-based question. Consider what you already know about this topic. How would you answer the question if you had no documents to examine?

2. Read each document carefully, underlining key phrases and words that address the document-based question. You may also wish to use the margin to make brief notes. Answer the questions that follow each document before moving on to the next document.

3. Based on your own knowledge and on the information found in the documents, formulate a thesis that directly answers the document-based question.

4. Organize supportive and relevant information into a brief outline.

5. Write a well-organized essay proving your thesis. You should present your essay logically. Include information both from the documents and from your own knowledge beyond the documents.

Question: Which economic, political, and social forces were most responsible for the new imperialism of the late nineteenth and early twentieth centuries?

PART A The following documents provide information about the causes of the new imperialism. Examine each document carefully. In the space provided, answer the question or questions that follow each document.

(continued)

DBQ 15: NEW IMPERIALISM: CAUSES

Document 1

In this excerpt, author Parker T. Moon pointed out which groups were most interested in imperialism.

> The makers of cotton and iron goods have been very much interested in imperialism. This group of import interests has been greatly strengthened by the demand of giant industries for colonial raw materials. . . . Shipowners demand coaling stations for their vessels and naval bases for protection. To these interests may be added the makers of armaments and of uniforms. The producers of telegraph and railway material and other supplies used by the government in its colony may also be included. . . . Finally, the most powerful business groups are the bankers. Banks make loans to colonies and backward countries for building railways and steamship lines. . . .

Source: Parker T. Moon, *Imperialism and World Politics*, Macmillan, 1936 (adapted)

Which groups were seeking colonies, according to this author? Explain each group's reason.

_____

_____

_____

_____

Document 2

This excerpt was written by American Senator A.J. Beveridge in 1898.

> American factories are making more than the American people can use; American soil is producing more than they can consume. Fate has written our policy for us; the trade of the world must and shall be ours. . . . We will establish trading posts throughout the world as distributing points for American products. We will cover the ocean with our merchant marines. We will build a navy to the measure of our greatness. . . .

According to Senator Beveridge, why should America become imperialistic?

_____

_____

_____

(continued)

DBQ 15: NEW IMPERIALISM: CAUSES

Document 3

This excerpt suggests another cause for imperialism.

> . . . [N]one of the colonial undertakings was motivated by the quest for capitalist profits; they all originated in political ambitions . . . the nations' will to power . . . [or] glory or national greatness.

Source: Raymond Aron, *The Century of Total War*, Doubleday & Co., 1954 (adapted)

What did this author say was the cause of imperialism?

_____

_____

_____

Document 4

Cecil Rhodes was a successful British imperialist in Africa. This excerpt is adapted from his position on imperialism.

> I contend that we [Britons] are the finest race in the world, and the more of the world we inhabit, the better it is for the human race. . . . It is our duty to seize every opportunity of acquiring more territory and we should keep this one idea steadily before our eyes that more territory simply means more of the Anglo-Saxon race, more of the best, the most human, most honourable race the world possesses.

Source: Cecil Rhodes, *Confession of Faith*, originally written at Oxford, 1877 (adapted)

According to Rhodes, why should Britain pursue a policy of imperialism?

_____

_____

_____

_____

(continued)

DBQ 15: NEW IMPERIALISM: CAUSES

Document 5

This excerpt suggests another reason for imperialism.

> But the economic side . . . must not be allowed to obscure [hide] the other factors. Psychologically speaking, . . . evolutionary teaching [about the "survival of the fittest"] was perhaps most crucial. It not only justified competition and struggle but introduced an element of ruthlessness. . . .

Source: William L. Langer, *The Diplomacy of Imperialism,* Knopf, 1935 (adapted)

According to Langer, what was the nonecomonic reason for the new imperialism?

_____

_____

_____

Document 6

This excerpt is from Rudyard Kipling's poem "The White Man's Burden" (1899). It gives another explanation for imperialism.

> Take up the white man's burden
>
> Send forth the best ye breed
>
> Go bind your sons to exile
>
> To serve your captives' need;
>
> To wait, in heavy harness,
>
> On fluttered folk and wild
>
> Your new-caught, sullen peoples,
>
> Half-devil and half-child.

According to the poem, what was the "white man's burden"? _____

_____

_____

_____

(continued)

DBQ 15: NEW IMPERIALISM: CAUSES

Document 7

In this excerpt, President William McKinley explains why the United States took over the Philippines.

> We could not leave them to themselves. They were unfit for self-government.
> There was nothing left for us to do but to take them over. Then we would be
> able to educate the Filipinos. We could uplift and civilize and Christianize
> them. . . .

Source: General James Rusling, "Interview with President William McKinley," *The Christian Advocate*, 1903 (adapted)

How did President McKinley justify the U.S. takeover of the Philippines?

_____

_____

_____

_____

Document 8

This excerpt gives another reason why Europeans were able to increase their colonial holdings. This is from a letter sent by Phan Thanh Gian, governor of a Vietnamese state, to his administrators in 1867.

> Now, the French are come, with their powerful weapons of war, to cause
> dissension among us. We are weak against them; our commanders and our
> soldiers have been vanquished. . . . The French have immense warships,
> filled with soldiers and armed with huge cannons. No one can resist them.
> They go where they want, the strongest ramparts fall before them.

Source: Phan Thanh Gian, retranslation from *Focus on World History: The Era of the First Global Age and Revolution*, Walch Publishing, 2002 (adapted)

How did this Vietnamese man explain the French imperialism in Indochina in 1867?

_____

_____

_____

(continued)

DBQ 15: NEW IMPERIALISM: CAUSES

Document 9

This map details European Imperialism in Africa in 1914.

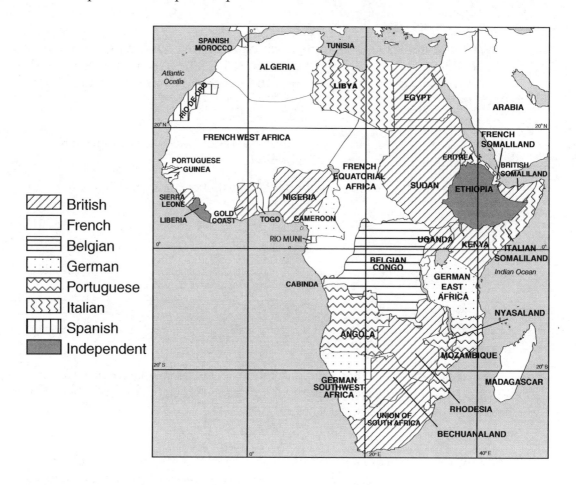

British
French
Belgian
German
Portuguese
Italian
Spanish
Independent

What cause for imperialism is evident in this map of Africa? Explain.

_____

_____

_____

_____

PART B

Which economic, political, and social forces were most responsible for the new imperialism of the late nineteenth and early twentieth centuries?

DBQ 15: TEACHER PAGE

Grading Key

Document 1

The author pointed out many economic causes for imperialism. Specifically, he pointed to the producers of cotton and iron, who needed markets; the importers, who could provide raw materials to the industries; the shipowners, who needed fueling stations; the weaponsmakers and others who supplied the government; and the bankers, who made loans to colonies for building railroads and steamship lines that serviced the colonies.

Document 2

Senator Beveridge suggested that the United States was destined to expand its trading because it was producing so much. Also, he suggested that it would be a sign of American power if the United States built a merchant marine, a navy, and a trading empire.

Document 3

According to Aron, economics (profit) was not the cause of imperialism; rather, the cause of imperialism was political. Countries were motivated by nationalism—a desire for power and glory.

Document 4

Rhodes believed that the British were a superior race and that it was their duty to acquire as much land as possible. As a result, there would be more Anglo-Saxons, the best race, controlling the world. This is a racist cause for imperialism.

Document 5

Langer said economic forces should not mask the other factors that caused imperialism. He pointed to Social Darwinism—the survival of the fittest—as the Europeans' justification for taking colonies.

Document 6

According to the poem, it was the white man's burden to help care for the "half-devil and half-child," Kipling's description of the people in the colonies. The poem illustrates the racial superiority that some white people felt at that time in history.

(continued)

Document 7

President McKinley said it was the responsibility of the United States to educate, uplift, civilize, and Christianize the Filipinos because they were "unfit" to rule themselves. This is another example of the racist viewpoint.

Document 8

This Vietnamese leader believed that the French were able to colonize the area because they had superior weapons and ships.

Document 9

This map shows how the Europeans (French, British, Belgians, Germans, Italians, Portuguese, and Spanish) carved up Africa. It shows the power of the Europeans to carry out imperialism.

Additional Information Beyond the Documents

These documents provide students with only fragments of evidence. Answers should include relevant information beyond the documents—information that students have learned from their classroom study. The following list suggests some of the information from outside learning that students might include in their essays.

- Maps of Africa and Asia before and after imperialism

- Conditions in Europe that led to imperialism—the Industrial Revolution, missionaries, and so forth.

- Political, social, and economic conditions in Africa and Asia before the Europeans arrived

DBQ 16: IMPERIALISM IN INDIA: AN EVALUATION

Historical Context

European imperialism was widespread in the late nineteenth and the twentieth centuries. It resulted in the carving up of areas of Africa and Asia into vast colonial empires. This was the case for British colonialism in India. As imperialism spread, the colonizer and the colony viewed imperialism differently. They saw both positive and negative effects of imperialism.

■ **Directions:** The following question is based on the accompanying documents in Part A. As you analyze the documents, take into account both the source of each document and the author's point of view. Be sure to do each of the following steps:

1. Carefully read the document-based question. Consider what you already know about this topic. How would you answer the question if you had no documents to examine?

2. Read each document carefully, underlining key phrases and words that address the document-based question. You may also wish to use the margin to make brief notes. Answer the questions that follow each document before moving on to the next document.

3. Based on your own knowledge and on the information found in the documents, formulate a thesis that directly answers the document-based question.

4. Organize supportive and relevant information into a brief outline.

5. Write a well-organized essay proving your thesis. You should present your essay logically. Include information both from the documents and from your own knowledge beyond the documents.

> **Question: What were the positive and negative effects of imperialism for Great Britain (the mother country) and for India (the colony)?**

The following documents provide information about the effects of imperialism on India. Examine each document carefully. In the space provided, answer the question or questions that follow each document.

(continued)

DBQ 16: IMPERIALISM IN INDIA: AN EVALUATION

Document 1

This excerpt points out the positive and negative results of imperialism.

> Modern progressive nations [European colonizers] . . . seek to control "garden spots" in the tropics. Under their direction, these places can yield the tropical produce that their citizens need. In return the progressive nations bring to the people of those garden spots the foodstuffs and manufactures they need. They develop the territory by building roads, canals, railways, and telegraphs. The progressive nations can establish schools and newspapers for the people of the colonies. They can also give these people the benefit of other blessings of civilization which they have not the means of creating themselves.

Source: O.P. Austin, "Does Colonization Pay?" *The Forum*, 1900 (adapted)

According to this author, what are the benefits of imperialism to the colony?

_____

What are the benefits of imperialism to the colonizer? _____

_____

Document 2

In this speech, Dadabhai Naoroji, an Indian, describes the effect of imperialism on India.

> To sum up the whole, the British rule has been—morally, a great blessing; politically, peace and order on one hand . . . on the other, materially, impoverishment. . . . The natives call the British system . . . "the knife of sugar." That is to say there is no oppression, it is all smooth and sweet, but it is the knife, nevertheless.

In these later comments, Naoroji stresses the negative aspects.

> Europeans [the British] occupy almost all the higher places in every department of government. . . . Natives, no matter how fit, are deliberately kept out of the social institutions started by Europeans. . . . All they [the Europeans] do is live off of India while they are here. When they go, they carry all they have gained.

Source: Dadabhai Naoroji, *Essays, Speeches, Addresses and Writings*, Caxton Printing Works, 1887 (adapted)

(continued)

DBQ 16: IMPERIALISM IN INDIA: AN EVALUATION

How is British imperialism both positive and negative for India, according to Naoroji?

_____

_____

_____

_____

Document 3

This excerpt comments on benefits to India during British imperialism.

> Englishmen . . . have given the people of India the greatest human blessing—
> peace. They have introduced Western education. This has brought an ancient
> and civilized nation in touch with modern thought, modern sciences, and
> modern life. They have built an administration that is strong and efficient.
> They have framed wise laws and have established courts of justice.

Source: Romesh Dutt, *The Economic History of India Under Early British Rule*, K. Paul,
    Trench, Trübner & Co. Ltd, 1902 (adapted)

What benefits has India gained during British imperialism, according to Dutt?

_____

_____

_____

Document 4

This excerpt describes additional benefits of imperialism.

> British brains, British enterprise, and British capital have changed the face of
> India. Means of communication have been developed. There are great
> numbers of bridges, more than 40,000 miles of railway, and 70,000 miles of
> paved roads. These testify to the skill and industry of British engineers.
> Irrigation works on a very large scale have brought 30 million acres under
> cultivation. This has greatly added to the agricultural wealth of the country.
> Industrialization has also begun. India now has improved sanitation and a
> higher standard of living. It has a fine transport system and carefully
> thought-out schemes for relief work. Because of these things famines have
> now almost disappeared.

Source: J.A.R. Marriott, *The English in India*, Clarendon Press, 1932 (adapted)

(continued)

DBQ 16: IMPERIALISM IN INDIA: AN EVALUATION

List at least five benefits of imperialism cited by this author.

_____

_____

_____

_____

_____

_____

Document 5

This excerpt points out the social and economic impact of imperialism on India.

> British rule brought with it from the West certain standards of humanity that Indian society had not yet reached. Early action was taken to stop infanticide [the killing of female babies]. . . . The slave trade was ended and the owning of slaves was forbidden. . . . One result of the new order was a steady rise in the value of India's export trade.

Source: Sir Reginald Coupland, *India: A Restatement*, 1945 (adapted)

What benefits of imperialism does this author identify?

_____

_____

_____

_____

(continued)

DBQ 16: IMPERIALISM IN INDIA: AN EVALUATION

Document 6

This excerpt explains how India became a "typical" colonial economy.

> This process continued throughout the nineteenth century. Other old Indian industries—shipbuilding, metalwork, glass, paper—and many crafts were broken up. Thus the economic development of India was stopped and the growth of new industry was prevented. . . . A typical colonial economy was built up. India became an agricultural colony of industrial England.
>
> It supplied raw materials and provided markets for England's industrial goods. The destruction of industry led to unemployment on a vast scale. . . . The poverty of the country grew. The standard of living fell to terribly low levels.

Source: Jawaharlal Nehru, *The Discovery of India*, The John Day Company, 1946 (adapted)

What negative effects of imperialism does Nehru point out? _____

_____

_____

_____

Document 7

In this excerpt, Mohandas Gandhi offers a complaint about imperialism.

> You English committed one supreme crime against my people. For a hundred years you have done everything for us. You have given us no responsibility for our own government.

What is Gandhi's criticism of imperialism? _____

_____

PART B

What were the positive and negative effects of imperialism for Great Britain (the mother country) and for India (the colony)?

Grading Key

Document 1

The colony benefits from imperialism because it receives food and manufactured goods. Roads, canals, railways, and schools are additional "blessings of civilization" that the colony receives. The colonizer receives tropical produce from the "garden spot."

Document 2

This Indian speaker refers to the British colonial rule as a "knife of sugar." Indians enjoyed peace and order, but they suffered from material poverty. In the second extract, the author points out that the British held all the high government positions and lived off of India.

Document 3

Dutt pointed out several benefits enjoyed by India—Western education and modern sciences, thought, and life. The British also built a strong, efficient government and provided wise laws as well as a judicial system.

Document 4

Benefits include the following: communication and transportation systems, an irrigation system that increased farmland and agricultural production, improved sanitary systems, and a social welfare system. As a result of British rule, Indians enjoyed a higher standard of living than previously.

Document 5

This British author identifies the "standards of humanity" that the British brought to India. These included the end of female infanticide, slavery, and the slave trade. Also, India's export trade increased in value.

Document 6

Indian economic development was disrupted when the British broke up old Indian industries and craft enterprises. India supplied raw materials and agricultural products for England, and India was a market for British industrial products. As a result, unemployment and poverty rose greatly in India.

(continued)

Document 7

Gandhi complains that Indians have not been allowed to develop the skills needed for self-government.

Additional Information Beyond the Documents

These documents provide students with only fragments of evidence. Answers should include relevant information beyond the documents—information that students have learned from their classroom study. The following list suggests some of the information from outside learning that students might include in their essays.

- Conditions in India before and during British imperialism

- Reasons for opposition to imperialism

DBQ 17: IMPERIALISM IN AFRICA: AN EVALUATION

Historical Context

European imperialism was widespread in the late nineteenth and twentieth centuries. It resulted in the carving up of areas of Africa and Asia into vast colonial empires. This was true for most of the continent of Africa. As imperialism spread, the colonizer and the colony viewed imperialism differently. They saw both positive and negative effects of imperialism.

■ **Directions:** The following question is based on the accompanying documents in Part A. As you analyze the documents, take into account both the source of each document and the author's point of view. Be sure to do each of the following steps:

1. Carefully read the document-based question. Consider what you already know about this topic. How would you answer the question if you had no documents to examine?

2. Read each document carefully, underlining key phrases and words that address the document-based question. You may also wish to use the margin to make brief notes. Answer the questions that follow each document before moving on to the next document.

3. Based on your own knowledge and on the information found in the documents, formulate a thesis that directly answers the document-based question.

4. Organize supportive and relevant information into a brief outline.

5. Write a well-organized essay proving your thesis. You should present your essay logically. Include information both from the documents and from your own knowledge beyond the documents.

The following documents provide information about the effects of imperialism on Africa. Examine each document carefully. In the space provided, answer the question or questions that follow each document.

(continued)

DBQ 17: IMPERIALISM IN AFRICA: AN EVALUATION

Document 1

This excerpt identifies negative aspects of imperialism.

> The period of imperialism has witnessed many wars. Most of these wars have been caused by attacks of white races upon so-called "lower races." They have resulted in the taking of territory by force. . . . The white rulers of the colonies live at the expense of the natives. Their chief work is to organize labor for their support. In the typical colony, the most fertile lands and the mineral resources are owned by white foreigners. These holdings are worked by natives under their direction. The foreigners take wealth out of the country. All the hard work is done by natives.

Source: J.A. Hobson, *Imperialism*, Allen and Unwin, 1902 (adapted)

What negative aspects of imperialism did this British scholar point out?

_____

_____

_____

_____

Document 2

Sékou Touré, an African nationalist, pointed out another negative aspect of imperialism.

> Colonialism's greatest misdeed was to have tried to strip us of our responsibility in conducting our own affairs and convince us that our civilization was nothing less than savagery, thus giving us complexes which led to our being branded as irresponsible and lacking in self-confidence.

What criticism of imperialism did this African nationalist offer?

_____

_____

_____

(continued)

DBQ 17: IMPERIALISM IN AFRICA: AN EVALUATION

Document 3

The All-African People's Conference was held in Accra, Ghana, in 1958. Its resolution "condemns colonialism and imperialism" based on the following premises.

> Whereas all African peoples everywhere strongly deplore the economic exploitation of African people by imperialist countries, thus reducing Africans to poverty in the midst of plenty. . . .
>
> Whereas fundamental human rights, freedom of speech, freedom of association, freedom of movement, freedom of worship, freedom to live a full and abundant life . . . are denied to Africans through the activities of imperialists.

For what reasons did this group condemn imperialism?

_____

_____

_____

_____

_____

Document 4

British Geographer and author, George H. T. Kimble, gave his point of view in a 1962 *New York Times Magazine* article.

> . . . [The colonial powers] failed to provide the African with sufficient [preparation]. . . . None of the newly independent countries had enough skilled African administrators to run their own [government] . . . [or] enough African technicians to keep the public utilities working. . . . And no country had an electorate that knew what independence was all about. . . . For all its faults, colonial government provided security of person and property in lands that had known little of either. . . . It was the colonial powers who were largely responsible for the opening of the region to the lumberman, miner, planter, and other men of means without whom its wealth would be continued to lie fallow [uncultivated].

Source: George H.T. Kimble, *The New York Times Magazine*, "Colonialism: The Good, the Bad, the Lessons," 1962 (adapted)

(continued)

DBQ 17: IMPERIALISM IN AFRICA: AN EVALUATION

What did this author cite as negative effects of imperialism?

_____

_____

What did the author cite as positive effects of imperialism? _____

_____

_____

Document 5

This is an African proverb.

> When the whites came to our country, we had the land and they had the Bible; now we have the Bible and they have the land.

What does this proverb imply about the effect of imperialism in Africa?

_____

_____

Document 6

This poem describes negative aspects of imperialism.

The White Man killed my father,	My brother was strong.
My father was proud.	His hands red with black blood
The White Man seduced my mother,	The White Man turned to me;
My mother was beautiful.	And in the Conqueror's voice said,
The White Man burnt my brother beneath the noonday sun,	"Boy! a chair, a napkin, a drink."

Source: David Diop, *An Anthology of West African Verse,* Ibadan University Press, 1957 (adapted)

What negative aspects of imperialism does David Diop present in this poem?

_____

_____

(continued)

DBQ 17: IMPERIALISM IN AFRICA: AN EVALUATION

Document 7

This excerpt points out other negative aspects of imperialism.

> The struggle for colonies does not result only in cash losses. There were also lives lost, wars fought, and hatreds aroused which threatened new wars. . . . Italy's trade with her colonies in 1894–1932 was worth 5,561 million lire [about $1,100 million]. This was less than one percent of her total foreign trade in the same period. In fact her expenditures on colonies for that time was 6,856 million lire. Obviously colonies cost more than they are worth in trade.

Source: Grover Clark, *Balance Sheets of Imperialism*, Columbia University Press, 1936 (adapted)

What evidence did this author provide to show that colonies were a negative financial drain on the Europeans?

_____

_____

_____

_____

PART B Evaluate the new imperialism of the late nineteenth and early twentieth centuries in Africa. What were the positive and negative effects of imperialism for the colonizer and the colony?

Grading Key

Document 1

Hobson pointed out the negative aspects of imperialism. There were many wars as the white races took over the territory of the "lower races" by force. The whites also took the most fertile land and the mines, and used the native people for labor. The foreigners took the wealth out of the country.

Document 2

Under imperialism, Africans had no responsibility for their government and became convinced that they were inferior. As a result, they were viewed as irresponsible and not self-confident.

Document 3

The conference resolution stated that imperialism should be condemned because it exploited African people and reduced them to poverty. Also, the imperialists denied the Africans freedom of speech, movement, worship, and association.

Document 4

This writer suggested that colonial people were not prepared for self-government and for running their countries' industries. On the positive side, the Europeans provided the Africans with protection. The colonial powers also opened up the resources of Africa that the Africans lacked the money to develop.

Document 5

The proverb says that the Africans lost their land to the whites. The Africans got a new religion, Christianity, in return. It implies that the Africans lost more than they gained.

Document 6

This poem lists all that was taken from the African by the white man—lives, labor, and pride. The white man treated the African like a child.

(continued)

DBQ 17: TEACHER PAGE

Document 7

The author points out that imperialism was expensive for the colonizer. The European countries lost money and lives in the wars fought over colonial claims. Expenditures for colonies exceeded the trade benefits for European countries such as Italy.

Additional Information Beyond the Documents

These documents provide students with only fragments of evidence. Answers should include relevant information beyond the documents—information that students have learned from their classroom study. The following list suggests some of the information from outside learning that students might include in their essays.

- Maps of Africa

- African conditions under European rule

DBQ 18: CAUSES OF WORLD WAR I

Historical Context

At the turn of the twentieth century, Europe seemed to enjoy a period of peace and progress. Yet below the surface, several forces were at work that would lead Europe into the "Great War." One of these forces was nationalism, and it had an explosive effect in the Balkans. But nationalism was only one of the many causes of World War I. Historians and eyewitnesses have described those causes and have tried to assess the responsibility for the war.

■ **Directions:** The following question is based on the accompanying documents in Part A. As you analyze the documents, take into account both the source of each document and the author's point of view. Be sure to do each of the following steps:

1. Carefully read the document-based question. Consider what you already know about this topic. How would you answer the question if you had no documents to examine?

2. Read each document carefully, underlining key phrases and words that address the document-based question. You may also wish to use the margin to make brief notes. Answer the questions that follow each document before moving on to the next document.

3. Based on your own knowledge and on the information found in the documents, formulate a thesis that directly answers the document-based question.

4. Organize supportive and relevant information into a brief outline.

5. Write a well-organized essay proving your thesis. You should present your essay logically. Include information both from the documents and from your own knowledge beyond the documents.

Question: Who and/or what caused World War I?

PART A The following documents provide information on the causes of World War I. Examine each document carefully. In the space provided, answer the question or questions that follow each document.

(continued)

DBQ 18: CAUSES OF WORLD WAR I

Document 1

This graph provides information on the increasing amounts of money spent on armaments from 1890 through 1914.

Rise of Military Spending among Europe's Leading Powers

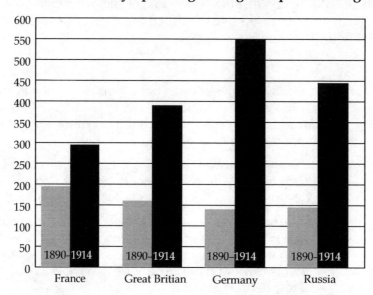

Source: James Killoran, Stuart Zimmer, Mark Jarrett, *Mastering Global History*, Jarrett Pub. Co., 1999 (adapted)

According to the graph, what change occurred between 1890 and 1914?

_____

_____

How did this change influence the coming of war?

_____

_____

_____

(continued)

DBQ 18: CAUSES OF WORLD WAR I

Document 2

This map of Europe on the eve of World War I shows the alliance systems.

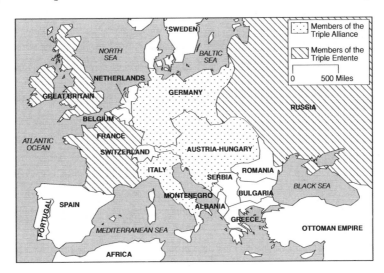

Who were the members of each alliance system? How did alliance systems contribute to the outbreak of World War I?

_____

_____

_____

Document 3

This excerpt outlines accusations against Serbia by Austria-Hungry.

> [T]he Royal Serbian Government has done nothing to repress these movements. It has permitted the criminal machinations of various societies and associations directed against the Monarchy, and has tolerated unrestrained language on the part of the press, the glorification of the perpetrators of outrages and the participation of officers and functionaries in subversive agitation. . . .
>
> . . . [The] Royal Government see themselves compelled to demand from the Royal Serbian Government a formal assurance that they condemn this dangerous propaganda against the Monarchy. . . .
>
> . . . To accept the collaboration in Serbia of representatives of the Austro-Hungarian Government for the suppression of the subversive movement . . .

Source: *Austro-Hungarian Red Book No. 7*, 1914 (adapted)

(continued)

DBQ 18: CAUSES OF WORLD WAR I

What accusations did Austria-Hungary make against Serbia?

_____

_____

_____

_____

What two demands did Austria-Hungary make on Serbia?

_____

_____

_____

_____

Document 4

This excerpt is from Article 231 of the Versailles Treaty, which Germany signed in 1919, thereby ending World War I.

> The Allied and Associate Governments affirm and Germany accepts the responsibility of Germany and her allies for causing all the loss and damage. . . .

According to the Versailles Treaty, who was responsible for World War I? _____

_____

Why did Germany agree to this article of the treaty? _____

_____

_____

(continued)

DBQ 18: CAUSES OF WORLD WAR I

Document 5

Count Brockdorff-Rantzau led the German delegation to the Versailles Peace Conference. On May 7, 1919, he protested some terms of the treaty. Here is an excerpt.

> It is demanded of us that we shall confess ourselves to be alone guilty of the war. Such a confession from my lips would be a lie. We are far from declining all responsibility for the fact that this great World War took place or that it was fought in the way that it was. . . . But we energetically deny that Germany and its people, who were convinced that they fought a war of defense, were alone guilty. No one would want to assert that the disaster began only at that disastrous moment when the successor of Austria-Hungary fell a victim to murderous hands. In the last fifty years, the imperialism of all European states has chronically poisoned international relations. Policies of retaliation, policies of expansion, and disregard for the right of peoples to determine their own destiny have contributed to the European malady which came to a crisis in the World War. The mobilization of Russia deprived statesmen of the opportunity of curing the disease, and placed the issue in the hands of the military powers.

What position did the German delegation leader present?

_____

_____

What did he say caused the war? _____

_____

_____

Document 6

In this excerpt, author Sidney Bradshaw Fay states his position on the causes of World War I.

> Nevertheless, a European war broke out. Why? Because in each country [of Europe] political and military leaders did certain things which lead to the mobilization [of their armies for war] and [finally] to the declarations of war, or [these leaders] failed to do certain things which might have prevented [the war]. In this sense, all the European countries in greater or lesser degree were responsible [for the outbreak of World War I].

Source: Sidney Bradshaw Fay, *Origins of the World War*, Macmillan, 1928 (adapted)

(continued)

DBQ 18: CAUSES OF WORLD WAR I

According to this author, who was responsible for the outbreak of World War I?

_____

What did he cite as evidence to support this claim? _____

_____

Document 7

This excerpt describes factors that contributed to World War I.

> The rise of Germany, whose supremacy France dreaded and whose navy
> menaced [threatened] England, had created among [England and France] an
> alliance which claimed it was defensive in nature but was denounced by
> German propaganda as an attempt at [the] encirclement [of Germany]. The
> two armed camps alarmed each other, and each grew heavy with multiplied
> incidents, which spread East [with the assassination of the Archduke
> Ferdinand], where Russia and Austria were advancing contradictory claims.

Source: Raymond Aron, *The Century of Total War*, Doubleday & Co., 1954 (adapted)

What responsibility did the alliance systems play in the outbreak of the war, according
to Aron?

_____

_____

What role did the assassination and the following ultimatum play in the outbreak
of the war?

_____

_____

 PART B   Who and/or what caused World War I?

Grading Key

Document 1

According to this chart, Germany, Great Britain, and Russia spent the most per person on armaments. The money spent on armies and navies meant that these countries were prepared for war. This led to an arms race and fear among neighboring countries.

Document 2

The map shows that there were two alliance systems. The Triple Entente included Russia, France, and Great Britain. The Triple Alliance included Germany, Austria-Hungary, and Italy. The alliances produced two armed camps, ready for war.

Document 3

The Austrian ultimatum accused Serbia of doing nothing to control groups that were criticizing and acting against the Austrian monarchy. The Austrian government demanded that the Serbian government condemn the propaganda against Austria and work with the Austro-Hungarian government to investigate and suppress the "subversive" groups in Serbia.

Document 4

According to the Versailles Treaty, Germany was responsible. Germany lost the war and had to accept the terms given in the treaty.

Document 5

He said that Germany alone was not to blame. It was fighting a defensive war. He said the cause of the war was "imperialism of all European states," which led to conflict. When the Russians mobilized, military men took over and diplomacy faded.

Document 6

Fay believed all of the European countries were to blame for the war. The leaders either took steps that led to war or failed to take steps that might have prevented the war.

(continued)

Document 7

Aron believed it was the alliance systems that brought on the war. Germany's rise in power threatened France and England, who joined together in a defensive alliance. Germany saw itself encircled by enemies. Therefore, when the assassination occurred, followed by the ultimatum, the countries that already had conflicts were pulled into war.

Additional Information Beyond the Documents

These documents provide students with only fragments of evidence. Answers should include relevant information beyond the documents—information that students have learned from their classroom study. The following list suggests some of the information from their outside learning that students might include in their essays.

- Nationalism among the subject nationalities in the Austro-Hungarian Empire and among European countries

- Imperialism and economic rivalries among European nations

- Alliance systems, militarism, the assassination of Archduke Franz Ferdinand, and the ultimatum

DBQ 19: WORLD WAR II: THE ROAD TO WAR

Historical Context

The 1920s began with a favorable outlook for peace. However, toward the end of the decade and throughout the 1930s, the clouds of war were forming. Dictators arose in countries that were dissatisfied with the results of World War I. Germany, Italy, and Japan took aggressive actions. Neither the League of Nations nor the democratic countries were able or willing to stop them. British Prime Minister Chamberlain suggested that a policy of appeasement was the best way to deal with Germany's Hitler. Nations and their leaders took actions that moved Europe toward war. The debate over the causes of World War II provides different perspectives.

■ **Directions:** The following question is based on the accompanying documents in Part A. As you analyze the documents, take into account both the source of each document and the author's point of view. Be sure to do each of the following steps:

1. Carefully read the document-based question. Consider what you already know about this topic. How would you answer the question if you had no documents to examine?

2. Read each document carefully, underlining key phrases and words that address the document-based question. You may also wish to use the margin to make brief notes. Answer the questions that follow each document before moving on to the next document.

3. Based on your own knowledge and on the information found in the documents, formulate a thesis that directly answers the document-based question.

4. Organize supportive and relevant information into a brief outline.

5. Write a well-organized essay proving your thesis. You should present your essay logically. Include information both from the documents and from your own knowledge beyond the documents.

> **Question: Why did the world plunge into World War II in 1939? What is the most effective response to aggression—appeasement or collective security?**

PART A

The following documents provide information about the steps leading to World War II. Examine each document carefully. In the space provided, answer the question or questions that follow each document.

(continued)

DBQ 19: WORLD WAR II: THE ROAD TO WAR

Document 1

In this excerpt, Adolf Hitler explains some of his ideas.

> One blood demands one Reich. Never will the German nation have the moral right to enter into colonial politics until, at least, it includes its own sons within a single state. . . . Oppressed territories are led back to the bosom of a common Reich, not by flaming protests, but by a mighty sword.

Source: Adolf Hitler, *Mein Kampf*, 1925–26 (adapted)

What did Hitler suggest was needed for Germany? How would that lead to war?

_____

_____

_____

Document 2

Italy attacked Ethiopia in 1935. Haile Selassie, emperor of Ethiopia, asked the League of Nations for help in stopping the invasion. He asked for military sanctions. Here is part of his appeal to the League of Nations.

> God and history will remember your judgement. . . . It is us today. It will be you tomorrow.

According to Haile Selassie, who should stop the aggressors?

_____

_____

What would happen if the aggressors were not stopped? _____

_____

_____

(continued)

DBQ 19: WORLD WAR II: THE ROAD TO WAR

Document 3

Hitler promised to tear up the Versailles Treaty. One article of the treaty forbade German troops from entering the Rhineland, a buffer zone between Germany and France. Two headlines and articles from *The New York Times* of March 8, 1936, are excerpted below. They explain this issue from the German and the French points of view.

HITLER SENDS GERMAN TROOPS INTO RHINELAND

Berlin, March 7—Germany today cast off the last shackles fastened upon her by the Treaty of Versailles when Adolf Hitler, as commander-in-chief of the Reich defense forces, sent his new battalions into the Rhineland's demilitarized zone. . . . "After three years of ceaseless battle," Hitler concluded, "I look upon this day as marking the close of the struggle for German equality status and with that re-won equality the path is now clear for Germany's return to European collective cooperation."

PARIS APPEALS TO LEAGUE

Paris, March 7—France has laid Germany's latest treaty violation before the Council of the League of Nations. At the same time the French Government made it quite clear that there could be no negotiation with Germany . . . as long as a single German soldier remained in the Rhineland in contravention [violation] of Germany's signed undertakings [agreements]. . . . What is essential, in the French view, is that the German government must be compelled by diplomatic pressure first, and by stronger pressure if need be, to withdraw from the Rhineland.

Source: *The New York Times*, March 8, 1936 (adapted)

What action did Hitler take in defiance of the Versailles Treaty? How did he explain his action?

_____

_____

_____

What was the reaction in France? How might this have led to war?

_____

_____

_____

_____

(continued)

DBQ 19: WORLD WAR II: THE ROAD TO WAR

Document 4

German aggression continued in 1938. Britain, France, and Italy met with Hitler to discuss his demands for the Sudetenland, a section of Czechoslovakia. This radio broadcast by William Shirer describes what happened at this meeting.

> It took the Big Four just five hours and twenty-five minutes here in Munich today to dispel the clouds of war and come to an agreement over the partition of Czechoslovakia. There is to be no European war . . . the price of that peace is . . . the ceding by Czechoslovakia of the Sudeten territory to Herr Hitler's Germany. The German Führer gets what he wanted. . . . His waiting ten short days has saved Europe from a world war . . . most of the peoples of Europe are happy that they won't have to go marching off to war. . . . Probably only the Czechs . . . are not too happy. But there seems very little that they can do about it in face of all the might and power represented here.

Source: William Shirer, CBS broadcast, 1938 (adapted)

What happened at this Munich Conference, according to Shirer? What did he feel was the reaction in Czechoslovakia and in the rest of Europe?

_____

_____

_____

_____

Document 5

This excerpt is from a speech that British Prime Minister Neville Chamberlain gave to Parliament in 1938. In it, Chamberlain explains why he favored a policy of appeasement in dealing with Hitler at Munich.

> With a little good will and determination, it is possible to remove grievances and clear away suspicion. . . . We must try to bring these four nations into friendly discussion. If they can settle their differences, we shall save the peace of Europe for a generation.
>
> And, in *The Times* [London]: I shall not give up the hope of a peaceful solution. . . . We sympathize with a small nation faced by a big and powerful neighbor. But we cannot involve the whole British Empire in war simply on her account. If we have to fight, it must be on larger issues than that. . . . I am a man of peace. . . . Yet if I were sure that any nation had made up its mind to dominate the world by fear of its force, I should feel that it must be resisted. . . . But war is a fearful thing.

(continued)

DBQ 19: WORLD WAR II: THE ROAD TO WAR

Why did Chamberlain suggest appeasement? _____

_____

_____

Under what conditions would he fight? _____

_____

_____

Document 6

Winston Churchill disagreed with Chamberlain's policy of appeasement. In this speech to Parliament in 1938, Churchill warns England about following a policy of appeasement.

> I have always held the view that keeping peace depends on holding back the aggressor. After Hitler's seizure of Austria in March, I appealed to the government. I asked that Britain, together with France and other powers, guarantee the security of Czechoslovakia. If that course had been followed, events would not have fallen into this disastrous state. . . . [I]n time, Czechoslovakia will be swallowed by the Nazi regime. . . . I think of all the opportunities to stop the growth of Nazi power which have been thrown away. The responsibility must rest with those who have control of our political affairs. They neither prevented Germany from rearming, nor did they rearm us in time. They weakened the League of Nations. . . . Thus they left us in the hour of trial without a strong national defense or system of international security.

What strategy did Churchill suggest for keeping peace and stopping the growth of Nazi power?

_____

_____

In his opinion, what opportunities had been lost in the quest for peace? _____

_____

Who was responsible for these lost opportunities? _____

_____

_____

_____

(continued)

DBQ 19: WORLD WAR II: THE ROAD TO WAR

Document 7

This excerpt offers a critical view of the Munich Agreement.

> The Munich Agreement was a . . . desperate act of appeasement at the cost of the Czechoslovak state, performed by Chamberlain and French premier, Daladier, in the vain hope that it would satisfy Hitler's stormy ambition, and thus secure for Europe a peaceful future. We know today that it was unnecessary . . . because the Czech defenses were very strong . . . and because the German generals, conscious of Germany's relative weakness at that moment, were actually prepared to attempt to remove Hitler . . . had he continued to move toward war.

Source: George F. Kennan, *Russia and the West Under Lenin and Stalin,* Atlantic Little Brown, 1961 (adapted)

What are two reasons Kennan felt the Munich Agreement was unnecessary?

_____

_____

_____

Document 8

In this excerpt, British historian A.J.P. Taylor presents another point of view on appeasement.

> Can any sane man suppose . . . that other countries could have intervened by armed force in 1933 to overthrow Hitler when he had come to power by constitutional means and was apparently supported by a large majority of the German people? The Germans put Hitler in power; they were the only ones who could turn him out. Also the "appeasers" feared that the defeat of Germany would be followed by a Russian domination over much of Europe.

Source: A.J.P. Taylor, *The Origins of the Second World War,* Atheneum, 1965 (adapted)

What were two reasons used to explain why appeasement was logical at that time?

_____

_____

_____

_____

(continued)

DBQ 19: WORLD WAR II: THE ROAD TO WAR

Document 9

In this excerpt, the author argues that the discussion about stopping Hitler prior to 1939 was not an issue, for several reasons.

> . . . [N]either the people nor the government of [Britain and France] were conditioned to the idea of war. . . . Before September 1, 1939, Hitler had done nothing that any major power considered dangerous enough to warrant precipitating [starting] a major European war. Nor was there any existing coalition that could have opposed Hitler's massive forces. For Britain sought to appease Hitler [and] the French feared a repetition of the bloody sacrifices of 1914–1918. Stalin wanted an agreement with Hitler on partitioning Europe and the United States rejected all responsibility for Europe.

Source: Keith Eubank, *Origins of World War II,* Thomas Y. Crowell Co., 1969 (adapted)

What evidence did this historian give for his belief that Hitler would not have been stopped prior to 1939?

_____

_____

_____

_____

PART B

Why did the world plunge into World War II in 1939? What is the most effective response to aggression—appeasement or collective security?

Grading Key

Document 1

According to Hitler, Germany needed to unite all Germans under one government—the Reich. This should be accomplished by force—"the sword."

Document 2

Haile Selassie wanted the League of Nations to stop Italian aggression. If the aggressor was not stopped, the emperor said, it would attack other nations. The aggressor should not be appeased.

Document 3

Hitler moved his troops into the Rhineland in violation of the Treaty of Versailles. He said it was time for Germany to be treated as an equal to the rest of the countries of Europe and no longer as a defeated, punished nation. France went to the League of Nations and asked that Germany be removed from the Rhineland diplomatically or by "stronger pressure" if necessary. The "stronger pressure" may have involved armed conflict in the Rhineland, which could have led to a larger war.

Document 4

At the Munich Conference, the Big Four agreed to let Germany take the Sudetenland. According to Shirer, the Europeans were happy because war was avoided. The Czechs were not happy, but they couldn't resist in the face of the power present.

Document 5

Chamberlain suggested appeasement because he believed "good will and determination" could solve differences among countries peacefully. He said Britain could not fight to save a small country like Czechoslovakia. But he said he was willing to fight over big issues, such as fighting to stop a country that was using force to try to take over the world. However, he preferred diplomacy and appeasement.

Document 6

According to Churchill, the aggressor had to be stopped. Britain, France, and the other countries had to join together (collective security) to stop aggression. They should have stopped Hitler when he seized Austria and when he threatened Czechoslovakia. The responsibility for this "disastrous state" rested with the British government, which weakened the League of Nations, failed to prevent Germany from rearming, and did not build up national defenses. Appeasement does not work, according to Churchill. It only postpones the inevitable conflict that will come.

(continued)

Document 7

Kennan believed that appeasement was unnecessary because Czechoslovakia was strong enough to save itself. In addition, the German generals would have tried to overthrow Hitler if he had taken the nation to war at that time.

Document 8

Taylor defended appeasement. He said there was little basis for suggesting that the Germans would reject Hitler, since they had put him in power and supported him. In addition, the other European countries were worried about Russian expansion in Europe.

Document 9

Eubank claimed that the countries of Europe, especially Britain and France, were not willing to fight because Hitler had done nothing that would warrant a renewal of the "bloody sacrifices" of World War I. All the countries had other interests, and they were not willing to unite to stop Hitler.

Additional Information Beyond the Documents

These documents provide students with only fragments of evidence. Answers should include relevant information beyond the documents—information that students have learned from their classroom study. The following list suggests some of the information from outside learning that students might include in their essays.

- Causes of World War II—alliance system, hatred for the Versailles Treaty, weaknesses of the League of Nations (collective security)

- Hitler's basic ideas about race, *lebensraum*, and Germany's rightful place in the world

DBQ 20: THE COLD WAR BEGINS

Historical Context

Between 1945 and 1950, the wartime alliance between the United States and the Soviet Union broke down. The Cold War began. For the next forty years, relations between the two superpowers swung between confrontation and détente. Each tried to increase its worldwide influence and spread its competing economic and political systems. At times during this period, the competitors were at the brink of war.

■ **Directions:** The following question is based on the accompanying documents in Part A. As you analyze the documents, take into account both the source of each document and the author's point of view. Be sure to do each of the following steps:

1. Carefully read the document-based question. Consider what you already know about this topic. How would you answer the question if you had no documents to examine?

2. Read each document carefully, underlining key phrases and words that address the document-based question. You may also wish to use the margin to make brief notes. Answer the questions that follow each document before moving on to the next document.

3. Based on your own knowledge and on the information found in the documents, formulate a thesis that directly answers the document-based question.

4. Organize supportive and relevant information into a brief outline.

5. Write a well-organized essay proving your thesis. You should present your essay logically. Include information both from the documents and from your own knowledge beyond the documents.

> **Question: How did the Cold War begin, and what "weapons" were used to fight this war?**

The following documents provide information about the Cold War. Examine each document carefully. In the space provided, answer the question or questions that follow each document.

(continued)

DBQ 20: THE COLD WAR BEGINS

Document 1

This excerpt is adapted from Winston Churchill's "Iron Curtain" speech of March 5, 1946.

> From Stettin in the Baltic to Trieste in the Adriatic, an iron curtain has descended across the Continent. Behind that line lie all the capitals of the ancient states of Central and Eastern Europe. . . . All these famous cities and the populations around them lie in what I must call the Soviet sphere, and all are subject, in one form or another, not only to Soviet influence but to a very high and in some cases increasing measure of control from Moscow.

How was the "iron curtain" a dividing line?

_____

_____

_____

Document 2

This excerpt is adapted from President Truman's speech to Congress on March 12, 1947.

> I believe that it must be the policy of the United States to support free peoples who are resisting attempted subjugation [domination] by armed minorities or by outside pressures. . . . Should we fail to aid Greece and Turkey in this fateful hour, the effect will be far-reaching to the West. . . . We must take immediate and resolute action. I therefore ask the Congress to provide authority for assistance to Greece and Turkey in the amount of $400 million. . . . The seeds of totalitarian regimes are nurtured by misery and want. They spread and grow in the evil soil of poverty and strife. They reach their full growth when the hope of a people for a better life has died.

What policy did President Truman suggest in this speech? _____

_____

_____

_____

_____

(continued)

DBQ 20: THE COLD WAR BEGINS

Document 3

This excerpt is adapted from a speech by U.S. Secretary of State George Marshall on June 5, 1947. In it, he explained his plan for European recovery.

> I need to say that the world situation is very serious. . . . Europe must have a great deal of additional help, or face heavy economic, social, and political damage. This would have a harmful effect on the world at large. There are also possibilities of disturbances because of the desperation of the people concerned. The effect on the economy of the United States should be clear to all. So the United States should do whatever it can to help restore normal economic health to the world. Without this there can be no political stability or peace. Our policy is directed . . . against hunger, poverty, desperation and chaos [disorder]. Its purpose is to revive a working economy in the world.

Why did Secretary of State Marshall suggest this plan for European recovery?

_____

_____

_____

_____

Document 4

This excerpt is adapted from the North Atlantic Treaty. It was signed by the United States, Canada, and ten nations of Western Europe in 1949. It established the North Atlantic Treaty Organization, or NATO.

> The parties agree that an armed attack against one or more of them in Europe or in North America shall be considered as an attack against them all. They agree that if such an armed attack occurs, each of them will assist the party or parties so attacked. Each will immediately take whatever action it considers necessary to restore and maintain the security of the North Atlantic area. It will, if necessary, use armed force.

What was the purpose of NATO? _____

_____

_____

(continued)

DBQ 20: THE COLD WAR BEGINS

Document 5

The Soviet Union responded to NATO by creating its alliance, the Warsaw Pact. The map below shows Warsaw Pact and NATO member nations in 1955.

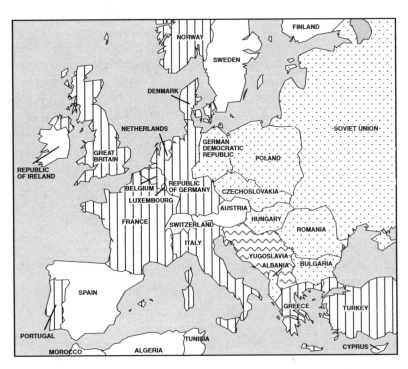

How did the Warsaw Pact "satellite" members provide a buffer for the Soviet Union?

_____

_____

_____

(continued)

DBQ 20: THE COLD WAR BEGINS

Document 6

This excerpt is adapted from a speech by Soviet Premier Nikita Khrushchev in 1956. In it, he explains his point of view about U.S. actions.

> The inspirers of the "cold war" began to establish military blocs—the North Atlantic bloc, SEATO, and the Baghdad pact. [They claim] they have united for defense against the "communist threat." But this is sheer hypocrisy! We know from history that when planning a redivision of the world, the imperialist powers have always lined up military blocs. Today the "anti-communism" slogan is being used as a smoke screen to cover up the claims of one power for world domination. The United States wants, by means of blocs and pacts, to secure a dominant position in the capitalist world. The inspirers of the "position of strength" policy assert that it makes another way impossible because it ensures a "balance of power" in the world. [They] offer the arms race as their main recipe for the preservation of peace! It is perfectly obvious that when nations compete to increase their military might, the danger of war becomes greater, not lesser. Capitalism will find its grave in another world war, should it unleash it.

What was Khrushchev's view of U.S. actions? According to Khrushchev, what would happen?

_____

_____

_____

_____

_____

_____

Document 7

The arms race was an important part of the Cold War. Both superpowers developed technology and used their nuclear power to build as many weapons as possible. This nuclear buildup led to a "balance of terror," which some saw as a deterrent to war. But others feared the use of these weapons. The charts on the next page show the buildup of ICBMs and long-range bombers between 1966 and 1974.

(continued)

DBQ 20: THE COLD WAR BEGINS

ICBMs and Long-Range Bombers, 1966–1974

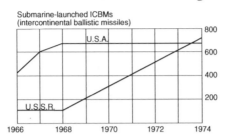

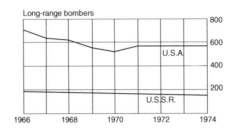

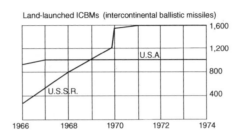

What impact did this arms race have on the world? _____

_____

_____

_____

_____

Document 8

The threat of nuclear war was obvious during the Cuban missile crisis of 1962. This excerpt is adapted from President John F. Kennedy's televised speech to the American people on October 22, 1962. It explains the position of the United States.

> We have unmistakable evidence that a series of offensive missile sites is now being built on that island. . . . Cuba has been made into an important strategic base by the presence of these long-range offensive weapons of sudden mass destruction. This is an open threat to the peace and security of all the Americas. Our objective must be to prevent the use of these missiles against this or any other country. We must secure their withdrawal from the Western Hemisphere. . . . I call upon Chairman Khrushchev to halt and eliminate this secret and reckless threat to world peace.

(continued)

DBQ 20: THE COLD WAR BEGINS

What was the basis for President Kennedy's demand that the missiles be removed from Cuba?

_____

_____

_____

Document 9

Kennedy ordered a quarantine of all offensive military equipment being sent into Cuba. Soviet Premier Khrushchev responded with this message.

> Mr. President, . . . the Soviet Government decided to render assistance to Cuba with the means of defense against aggression—only with means for defense purposes. . . . We have supplied them to prevent an attack on Cuba.
>
> I regard with respect and trust the statement you made in your message of October 27, 1962, that there would be no attack, no invasion of Cuba, and not only on the part of the United States, but also on the part of other nations in the Western Hemisphere. . . .
>
> It is for this reason that we instructed our officers . . . to take appropriate measures to discontinue construction of the aforementioned facilities, to dismantle them, and to return them to the Soviet Union.

How did Premier Khrushchev explain why missiles were placed in Cuba and why they could now be removed?

_____

_____

_____

_____

_____

PART B How did the Cold War begin, and what "weapons" were used to fight this war?

Grading Key

Document 1

Churchill stated that an "iron curtain," or a great division, now existed between Eastern and Western Europe. The East European governments were influenced and even controlled by the U.S.S.R.

Document 2

Truman proposed that the United States give $400 million in aid to Greece and Turkey to allow them to resist domination by outside pressures (Communists). This financial aid would remove the poverty and misery that plagued these countries after the war. As a result, their people would have hope for a better life, and they would not turn to communism.

Document 3

In order to protect its interests and to restore "economic health" to the world, the United States needed to help rebuild Europe so it could recover from the destruction suffered during the war. With U.S. aid, desperate Europeans would not turn to communism, and the United States would have European trading partners.

Document 4

NATO was established as a mutual defense pact. It would protect all members from Communist aggression. An armed attack on one would be considered as an armed attack on all.

Document 5

The Warsaw Pact countries, which were under Soviet control, served as a buffer between the U.S.S.R. and Western Europe.

Document 6

Khrushchev said the United States was setting up military blocs so that it could gain a dominant position in the capitalist world—not out of a fear of communism, as the United States had said. In addition, the arms race was supposed to result in a balance of power. But, according to Khrushchev, it could easily lead to war. Capitalism would end in "another world war" if it followed that path.

(continued)

Document 7

The illustrations show the rapid buildup of ICBMs and long-range bombers. The U.S.S.R. led in ICBMs in 1974. In contrast, the United States had more long-range bombers. The fear that either country might use these destructive nuclear weapons led to a balance of terror. This arms race led to dangerous competition between the two superpowers, which could have led to a nuclear war.

Document 8

The offensive missiles could destroy most cities in the Western Hemisphere. Consequently, Kennedy demanded that the Soviet Union remove these missiles from Cuba and end this "threat to world peace."

Document 9

Khrushchev agreed to remove the missiles because, he said, they were only put there to defend and protect Cuba from an attack. Since the United States had promised that Cuba would not be attacked by any country in the Western Hemisphere, the missiles were no longer needed. The world stepped back from the brink of war.

Additional Information Beyond the Documents

These documents provide students with only fragments of evidence. Answers should include relevant information beyond the documents—information that students have learned from their classroom study. The following list suggests some of the information from outside learning that students might include in their essays.

- Competing ideological systems

- Alliance systems

- Arms race

- Regional conflicts—Latin America, Vietnam, Korea, Berlin

- Use of propaganda and economic and military aid to gain influence around the world

- Containment, détente, and other policies of the United States and the Soviet Union

Name _____   Date _____

DBQ 21: DECOLONIZATION AND REVOLUTION
1945–1975

Historical Context

   After World War II, major independence movements emerged. Revolutions also occurred. Their shared goal was to change the leadership of countries such as India, Vietnam, Cuba, China, and Ghana. Demands for independence swept the colonies of Africa. At the same time, revolutions transformed Cuba and China. Strong leaders shaped these movements for independence and change.

■ **Directions:** The following question is based on the accompanying documents in Part A. As you analyze the documents, take into account both the source of each document and the author's point of view. Be sure to do each of the following steps:

   1. Carefully read the document-based question. Consider what you already know about this topic. How would you answer the question if you had no documents to examine?

   2. Read each document carefully, underlining key phrases and words that address the document-based question. You may also wish to use the margin to make brief notes. Answer the questions that follow each document before moving on to the next document.

   3. Based on your own knowledge and on the information found in the documents, formulate a thesis that directly answers the document-based question.

   4. Organize supportive and relevant information into a brief outline.

   5. Write a well-organized essay proving your thesis. You should present your essay logically. Include information both from the documents and from your own knowledge beyond the documents.

Question: What were the methods and roles of leaders and organizations in the movement for independence and change in the period between 1945 and 1975? Evaluate these methods and roles.

 PART A   The following documents provide information about the revolutions and independence movements that swept the world after World War II. Examine each document carefully. In the space provided, answer the question or questions that follow each document.

(continued)

DBQ 21: DECOLONIZATION AND REVOLUTION 1945–1975

Document 1

This excerpt is adapted from the "Declaration Against Colonialism," which was adopted by the United Nations in 1960.

> The General Assembly,
>
> Mindful of the determination proclaimed by the peoples of the world in the Charter of the United Nations to reaffirm faith in fundamental human rights, in the dignity and worth of the human person . . . , Solemnly proclaims the necessity of bringing to a speedy and unconditional end colonialism in all its forms . . . And to this end Declares that:
>
> 1. The subjection of peoples to alien subjugation, domination and exploitation . . . is contrary to the Charter of the United Nations and is an impediment to the promotion of world peace and co-operation.
>
> 2. All peoples have the right to self-determination; by virtue of that right they freely determine their political status and freely pursue their economic, social and cultural development.

What was the main idea of this U.N. declaration? _____

_____

_____

_____

Document 2

The following is an excerpt adapted from the Vietnamese Declaration of Independence, written by Ho Chi Minh in 1945.

> The whole Vietnamese people, animated by a common purpose, are determined to fight to the bitter end against any attempt by the French colonialists to reconquer their country.

What course of action did Ho Chi Minh recommend to the Vietnamese people?

_____

_____

(continued)

DBQ 21: DECOLONIZATION AND REVOLUTION
1945–1975

Document 3

This excerpt was written by Mahatma Gandhi. In this adaptation, he describes his method for fighting for the independence of India.

> Passive [nonviolent] resistance is a method of securing rights by personal suffering; it is the reverse of resistance by arms. . . . If I do not obey the law and accept the penalty for its breach [breaking], I use soul-force. It involves sacrifice of self.

Gandhi led the Salt March of 1930, in which he used passive resistance. In describing this protest, Gandhi said the following:

> If the awakening of the people in the country is true and real, the salt law is as good as abolished. [He then raised a lump of salt.] With this, I am shaking the foundations of the British Empire.

What method of working toward independence did Gandhi recommend to the Indian people?

_____

_____

_____

What was Gandhi's goal? _____

_____

_____

_____

(continued)

DBQ 21: DECOLONIZATION AND REVOLUTION 1945–1975

Document 4

These are the words of Nelson Mandela in 1994. He fought tirelessly for the end of apartheid in South Africa.

> During my lifetime I have dedicated myself to the struggle of the African People. I have cherished the ideal of a democratic and free society in which all persons live together in harmony and with equal opportunities. It is an ideal which I hope to live for and to achieve. But, if needs be, it is an ideal for which I am prepared to die.

What change did Mandela recommend for South Africa? Why? _____

_____

_____

_____

Document 5

Kwame Nkrumah was the leader in the fight for Ghana's independence. He described the movement with these words in 1965.

> Independence for the Gold Coast [Ghana] was my aim. It was a colony, and I have always regarded colonialism as the policy by which a foreign power binds territories to herself by political ties, with the primary object of promoting her own economic advantage.
>
> . . . Thus we have witnessed the greatest awakening ever seen on this earth of suppressed and exploited peoples against the powers that have kept them in subjection. This, without a doubt, is the most significant happening of the twentieth century.

What was the "most significant happening of the twentieth century," according to Nkrumah?

_____

_____

_____

(continued)

172

DBQ 21: DECOLONIZATION AND REVOLUTION 1945–1975

Why was he opposed to colonialism? _____

_____

_____

Document 6

Jomo Kenyatta was the leader of the fight for independence for Kenya. He became Kenya's first president. In 1964, he said the following about this fight.

> The land is ours. When Europeans came, they kept us back and took our land. The freedom tree can only grow when you pour blood on it.

Why did Kenyatta call for independence? _____

_____

_____

_____

Document 7

This excerpt is adapted from a speech given by Mao Zedong in 1945.

> Our aim . . . is to build up the confidence of the whole [Communist] Party and the entire people in the certain triumph of the revolution. . . . We must . . . raise the political consciousness of the entire people so that they may willingly and gladly fight together with us for victory. We should fire the whole people with the conviction that China belongs not to the reactionaries but to the Chinese people. . . . We firmly believe that, led by the Chinese Communist Party . . . the Chinese people will achieve complete victory.

What was Mao Zedong attempting to do in this speech? _____

_____

_____

What method of change did Mao recommend? _____

_____

_____

(continued)

DBQ 21: DECOLONIZATION AND REVOLUTION 1945–1975

Document 8

This excerpt is adapted from a speech Fidel Castro gave in his defense at a trial in 1953. In this speech, Castro rallied the support of the Cuban people to fight against the dictator.

> When we speak of struggle, the people means the vast unredeemed masses, to whom all make promises and whom all deceive; we mean the people who yearn for a better, more dignified and more just nation . . . people who, to attain these changes, are ready to give even the very last breath of their lives—when they believe in something or in someone. . . .
>
> These are the people, the ones who know misfortune and, therefore, are capable of fighting with limitless courage! To the people whose desperate roads through life have been paved with the bricks of betrayal we . . . say . . . Here you have it, fight for it with all your might so that liberty and happiness may be yours.

Which "people" did Fidel Castro feel were the basis of the Cuban Revolution?

_____

_____

_____

_____

_____

_____

 PART B What were the methods and roles of leaders and organizations in the movement for independence and change in the period between 1945 and 1975? Evaluate these methods and roles.

DBQ 21: TEACHER PAGE

Grading Key

Document 1

It called for an end to colonialism. It said that it is a fundamental human right for the people of a country to be free from control by another country. All people have the right to choose the government they want and to develop their own economy and culture.

Document 2

Ho Chi Minh urged the Vietnamese people to unite and fight to the end to prevent the French from regaining control of Vietnam.

Document 3

Gandhi urged the use of passive resistance: do not obey unjust laws, and accept the consequences. He used this method in the Salt March. He felt that if the Indian people refused to pay the salt tax, the British Empire would start to break up. India would gain independence by passive resistance. India would use peaceful means—"soul-force."

Document 4

Mandela, in his fight to end apartheid, was willing to die for his goal: that all people live together in a "democratic and free" society. It would mean the end of apartheid, which had separated and subjugated the blacks in South Africa.

Document 5

Nkrumah felt that the independence movement that was sweeping Africa was the most important event in the twentieth century. This movement would sweep away colonialism. Nkrumah was against colonialism because, he said, its primary purpose was to gain wealth for the foreign power while keeping the colonial people in subjection.

Document 6

Kenyatta claimed that the Europeans had taken the land that belonged to the people of Kenya, who must be willing to shed their blood to regain their independence. Kenyatta was motivating the people to fight.

(continued)

Document 7

Mao made the Chinese people aware of the need to fight together against the "reactionaries" (the Nationalists). Mao was raising the confidence of and predicting a victory for the Chinese people if they followed the leadership of the Communist Party.

Document 8

In this speech, Castro rallied the support of the Cuban people to fight against the dictator. The people were the masses who wanted a better, more just country. The people must be willing to fight and die for what they believe in. These people included the unemployed, the laborers, small businessmen, and young professionals who were not doing well under the dictator's regime. They must fight for liberty and happiness. It was their duty to be revolutionaries.

Additional Information Beyond the Documents

These documents provide students with only fragments of evidence. Answers should include relevant information beyond the documents—information that students have learned from their classroom study. The following list suggests some of the information from outside learning that students might include in their essays.

- Information about independence movements and methods

- Leaders for independence—Mandela, Ho Chi Minh, Gandhi, Kenyatta, Nkrumah

- Revolutionary leaders—Fidel Castro for the Cuban Revolution and Mao Zedong for the Chinese Revolution

- Methods used to motivate and fight for change and independence

DBQ 22: TWENTIETH-CENTURY CHINA

Historical Context

Two men shaped China during the second half of the twentieth century. Mao Zedong led his followers to victory in the Chinese Revolution in 1949. He then set up the People's Republic of China and introduced his brand of communism to the nation. After Mao's death in 1976, Deng Xiaoping emerged as the leader. He introduced his own program, the Four Modernizations, and started China's "Second Revolution."

■ **Directions:** The following question is based on the accompanying documents in Part A. As you analyze the documents, take into account both the source of each document and the author's point of view. Be sure to do each of the following steps:

1. Carefully read the document-based question. Consider what you already know about this topic. How would you answer the question if you had no documents to examine?

2. Read each document carefully, underlining key phrases and words that address the document-based question. You may also wish to use the margin to make brief notes. Answer the questions that follow each document before moving on to the next document.

3. Based on your own knowledge and on the information found in the documents, formulate a thesis that directly answers the document-based question.

4. Organize supportive and relevant information into a brief outline.

5. Write a well-organized essay proving your thesis. You should present your essay logically. Include information both from the documents and from your own knowledge beyond the documents.

Question: Which man should be most honored in modern Chinese history, Mao Zedong or Deng Xiaoping? To answer this question, take the following steps:

- Describe the social, economic, and political goals and policies of both Mao Zedong and Deng Xiaoping.

- Evaluate the impact each man had on China.

- Take a position in answer to the question, for a debate or a seminar. Explain your rationale.

(continued)

DBQ 22: TWENTIETH-CENTURY CHINA

 PART A The following documents provide information about China under the leadership of Mao Zedong and Deng Xiaoping. Examine each document carefully. In the space provided, answer the question or questions that follow each document.

Document 1

The following quotations are adapted from Mao Zedong's *Little Red Book* (1964).

> A revolution is not a dinner party, or painting a picture; it cannot be leisurely, gentle, kind, courteous, and restrained. A revolution is an act of violence by which one class overthrows another.
>
> Political power grows out of the barrel of a gun.
>
> Just because we have won a victory, we must never relax our vigilance [watchfulness] against the mad plots for revenge by the imperialists.

According to these quotations from Mao Zedong, what were his goals and methods?

_____

_____

Document 2

In this excerpt, Nien Cheng describes the experience of a friend during the Great Leap Forward.

> When Li Zhen [a Chinese teacher and friend of the author] returned to Shanghai, the city was suffering from a severe food shortage as a result of the catastrophic economic failure of the Great Leap Forward Campaign launched by Mao Zedong in 1958. Long lines of people were forming at dawn at Shanghai police stations, waiting to apply for exit permits to leave the country. This was such an embarrassment for the Shanghai authorities that they viewed Li Zhen's return from affluent Hong Kong to starving Shanghai as an opportunity for propaganda.

Source: Nien Cheng, *Life and Death In Shanghai*, Grove Press, 1987 (adapted)

What was the effect of the Great Leap Forward on the people? _____

_____

_____

(continued)

DBQ 22: TWENTIETH-CENTURY CHINA

Document 3

This excerpt from Nien Cheng describes the beginning of Mao's Cultural Revolution.

> Next day, I read in the newspaper that on August 18 Mao Zedong had reviewed the first contingent of the Red Guards in Beijing. . . . His special message to the Red Guards was to carry the torch of the Cultural Revolution to the far corners of China and to pursue the purpose of the Revolution to the very end. Young people all over China received the message from the man they had been brought up to worship as a call to arms. At the early stage of the Cultural Revolution the declared target was still only the "capitalist class," and it was there that the Red Guards focused their attack.

Source: Nien Cheng, *Life and Death In Shanghai*, Grove Press, 1987 (adapted)

How did the Red Guards view Mao? _____

What was Mao's message to the Red Guards? _____

_____

Who was the target of the Cultural Revolution in the beginning? _____

_____

Document 4

This adapted excerpt describes the Cultural Revolution in China.

> The Cultural Revolution began with a power struggle. Mao's leadership had been challenged by the Communist Party Congress; in May 1966 he struck back. He attacked moderates for lacking zeal, then targeted his rivals in the leadership. He called on millions of patriotic youths to form the Red Guards to "bombard the headquarters" of government and dislodge his opponents. What followed was a reign of terror. Marauding Red Guards hunted down "class enemies," smashed Buddhist temples and other so-called symbols of feudalism and effectively paralyzed China's government. The country sank close to civil war and worse.

Source: George Wehrfrite, "The Swing Pendulum," *Newsweek*, March 6, 1996

What were Mao's goals during the Cultural Revolution? _____

_____

_____

(continued)

DBQ 22: TWENTIETH-CENTURY CHINA

What was the impact of the Cultural Revolution on China? _____

_____

_____

Document 5

This excerpt offers one view of Mao.

> Mao was a TOTAL revolutionary. He didn't want to make peace with the system of feudalism and imperialism responsible for the suffering of the people. . . . Mao was a real communist: He fought for a world without classes and without oppressors. . . . He led the masses to wage armed struggle, to overthrow the system, and put the common people in charge of society. . . . Mao led the Great Proletarian Cultural Revolution which spread this truth to every corner of the world: It is right to rebel against reaction! . . . With Mao's leadership, people at the bottom in China became conscious revolutionizers of society. All kinds of new things were accomplished—things impossible under capitalism. In factories, hospitals, schools, farms, and in the arts—the masses developed new socialist ways of doing things and relating to each other. Never before in history did the masses of working people have so much power to change the world.

Source: "Mao Tse-tung: The Greatest Revolutionary of Our Time," Revolutionary Worker Online, http://rwor.org/a/china/mao.htm (adapted)

According to this selection, how should Mao be viewed in history? Why?

_____

_____

_____

_____

(continued)

DBQ 22: TWENTIETH-CENTURY CHINA

Document 6

This cartoon compares Mao and Deng.

Source: Brian Duffy, *The Des Moines Register*, 1985

According to the cartoon, how did the policies of Mao and Deng differ?

_____

_____

_____

(continued)

*Document-Based Assessment for
Global History*

DBQ 22: TWENTIETH-CENTURY CHINA

Document 7

These quotations are attributed to Chinese Communist leader, Deng Xiaoping.

> It doesn't matter whether the cat is black or white, so long as it catches mice.
>
> To get rich is glorious.
>
> If you open the window, some flies naturally get in.

According to these quotations, what was Deng's economic policy? _____

_____

_____

Document 8

This excerpt describing China's booming coastal provinces and economically depressed rural areas provides insight into the impact of both Mao and Deng on China.

> The party (Mao's Communist) offered an ideology open to all citizens. Yet the regime's own blunders have only deepened China's underlying fissures. The fanaticism of the Cultural Revolution (1966–1976) alienated ethnic minorities. The government misallocated resources to capital-intensive heavy industries and neglected agriculture. . . . State planning restricted the free flow of labor and capital, either across regions or from the countryside to cities. These policies kept people poor and doubled regional income disparities from 1952 to 1978.
>
> At first the reforms introduced by Deng Xiaoping reversed this trend. With market forces, not the government, channeling people and money, income disparities fell by 20% between 1979 and 1991. But Deng himself undermined this process with his famous call to "let some get rich first." In practice, this meant giving priority to the coast . . . . Private enterprise was encouraged. Foreign investors arrived en masse, pouring more than $300 billion into China in the 1990s. Within a decade the entire eastern seaboard had been transformed. At the same time, industrial decay spread throughout the northeast as Beijing dragged its heels on reforming state-owned enterprises. Progress in large agrarian provinces stalled as farmers could squeeze no more out of their land . . . By 1999, regional inequalities had returned to 1978 levels.

Source: Minxin Pei, *Newsweek International*, October 28, 2002 (adapted)

(continued)

DBQ 22: TWENTIETH-CENTURY CHINA

According to paragraph 1, what was Mao's impact on China? _____

_____

_____

_____

According to paragraph 2, how did Deng benefit and hurt China? _____

_____

_____

_____

_____

PART B   Which man should be most honored in modern Chinese history, Mao Zedong or Deng Xiaoping? To answer this question, take the following steps:

- Describe the social, economic, and political goals and policies of both Mao Zedong and Deng Xiaoping.

- Evaluate the impact each man had on China.

- Take a position in answer to the question, for a debate or a seminar. Explain your rationale.

For a seminar or debate, provide students with more information, such as additional cartoons and charts. To add more recent material, go to web sites such as China News Service (www.chinanews.cn). If you want to add other issues to the chapter, you might include information about convict or forced labor in China. For this, you might use excerpts from Harry Wu's book, *Bitter Winds*. China's handling of its population issues is another topic you might want to add to include.

Grading Key

Document 1

Mao's goal was to lead a revolution in which one class, the peasants and workers, overthrew another class, the wealthy. His method was violence and force, or guns.

Document 2

During the Great Leap Forward, an economic failure, the Chinese people suffered from severe food shortages. Many tried to leave China, which embarrassed the authorities.

Document 3

The Red Guards virtually worshiped Mao. Mao's message was to carry out the Cultural Revolution all over China. The target of in the beginning was the capitalists.

Document 4

During the Cultural Revolution, Mao was trying to regain full control of the government. To do this, he sent the Red Guards against his opponents. This resulted in a reign of terror in which Red Guards hunted down and eliminated "class enemies." As a result of the Cultural Revolution, China sank into chaos.

Document 5

This source views Mao as a real communist and hero. He led the masses in an armed struggle to overthrow the system and fought for a classless society. During the Great Proletarian Cultural Revolution, Mao spread the idea that revolution against reaction and capitalism was the way. The masses of working people gained the power to change the world.

(continued)

Document 6

Mao's policy in his *Little Red Book* was for communism—a sharing of the wealth. In contrast, Deng's policy was to make money for yourself.

Document 7

Deng's economic policy was to get rich for yourself. It didn't matter whether it was through capitalism or communism as long as the economy worked. He acknowledged that the needed economic changes would cause some problems.

Document 8

Under Mao, all citizens could participate, but the government misdirected resources and the Chinese people stayed poor. Deng's strategy brought in new people and wealth, but that wealth was limited to a few, with priority given to the coastal regions.

Additional Information Beyond the Documents

These documents provide students with only fragments of evidence. Essays should include relevant information beyond the documents—information that students have learned from their classroom study, outside reading and viewing, and other learning experiences. The following list suggests some of that information.

- Mao Zedong: leadership of the civil war against the Nationalists; establishment of the People's Republic of China with its economic, social, and political policies; Five Year Plans, Great Leap Forward, Great Proletarian Cultural Revolution

- Deng Xiaoping: reforms of the Four Modernizations; introduction of free-market economic features; political control by the government; jailing of opponents; forced labor camps; one-child policy

DBQ 23: HUMAN RIGHTS

Historical Context

In 1984, the United Nations Commission on Human Rights drafted the Universal Declaration of Human Rights. It defined basic human rights for people around the world. Some of the rights included are:

Article 1—All human beings are born free and equal in dignity and rights.

Article 3—Everyone has the right to life, liberty, and security of person.

Article 5—No one shall be subjected to torture or to cruel, inhuman, or degrading treatment or punishment.

Article 18—Everyone has the right to freedom of thought, conscience, and religion.

Article 19—Everyone has the right to freedom of opinion and expression.

Article 20—Everyone has the right to freedom of peaceful assembly and association.

Article 21—Everyone has the right to take part in the government of his country, directly or through freely chosen representatives.

During the more than fifty years since the signing of the declaration, human rights continue to be violated. Efforts by the United Nations, Amnesty International, and other human rights groups increase the awareness of these violations. These groups also attempt to stop the violations from happening.

■ **Directions:** The following question is based on the accompanying documents in Part A. As you analyze the documents, take into account both the source of each document and the author's point of view. Be sure to do each of the following steps:

1. Carefully read the document-based question. Consider what you already know about this topic. How would you answer the question if you had no documents to examine?

2. Read each document carefully, underlining key phrases and words that address the document-based question. You may also wish to use the margin to make brief notes. Answer the questions that follow each document before moving on to the next document.

3. Based on your own knowledge and on the information found in the documents, formulate a thesis that directly answers the document-based question.

4. Organize supportive and relevant information into a brief outline.

5. Write a well-organized essay proving your thesis. You should present your essay logically. Include information both from the documents and from your own knowledge beyond the documents.

(continued)

DBQ 23: HUMAN RIGHTS

Question: How have the human rights of three specific groups of people around the world been violated? What actions have been taken to stop each of these abuses? How effective have these actions been?

PART A

The following documents address various human rights abuses. Examine each document carefully. In the space provided, answer the question or questions that follow each document.

Document 1

This excerpt describes the violation of human rights in Cambodia.

> From the middle of 1975 to the end of 1978, between one million and three million Cambodians, out of a population of about seven million, died at the hands of Pol Pot's Khmer Rouge. Former government employees, army personnel, and "intellectuals" were executed in the hundreds of thousands. Others were killed by disease, exhaustion, and malnutrition during forced urban evacuations, migrations, and compulsory labor. Families were broken apart and communal living established; men and women were compelled to marry partners selected by the state. Education and religious practices were proscribed [forbidden].

Source: David Hawk, *The New Republic*, "The Killing of Cambodia," 1982 (adapted)

What human rights were violated during the Cambodian genocide?

_____

_____

_____

_____

_____

(continued)

DBQ 23: HUMAN RIGHTS

Document 2

This excerpt is from an interview with Cambodian Holocaust survivor, Dith Pran.

> MR. PRAN: And my mission as a survivor. I must do something to tell the world what happened to the two millions of Cambodian people that got killed during the Khmer Rouge.
>
> WILLIAMS: There's a new project, a book designed so people will never forget the genocide in Cambodia in the mid-1970s. It's the work of Dith Pran. . . . It was 1975 when Pol Pot's Khmer Rouge swept into Cambodia and launched a ruthless, genocidal campaign that eventually claimed an estimated two million lives. The story of one Cambodian inspired the movie *The Killing Fields* based on the life of Dith Pran. . . . Now Dith Pran, who's working in New York as a photographer for the *New York Times,* wants to make sure people never forget the genocide in Cambodia. He has compiled a collection of personal essays by survivors of the killing fields . . . that has become a book called *Children of Cambodia's Killing Fields.* The royalties from the book go to the Dith Pran Holocaust Awareness Project teaches American high school students about what happened in Cambodia.

Source: Brian Williams, MSNBC interview with Dith Pran, 1998 (adapted)

How did Dith Pran hope to help end genocide? _____

_____

_____

_____

Document 3

This is the text from a sign from South Africa.

> **FOR USE BY WHITE PERSONS**
>
> **THESE PUBLIC PREMISES AND THE AMENITIES THEREOF HAVE BEEN RESERVED FOR THE EXCLUSIVE USE OF WHITE PERSONS.**
>
> **By Order Provincial Secretary**

(continued)

DBQ 23: HUMAN RIGHTS

How did this sign violate human rights in South Africa? _____

_____

_____

_____

Document 4

Below is a time line of apartheid-related events in South Africa.

> 1964—Anti-apartheid leader Nelson Mandela is sentenced to life in jail.
>
> 1973—United Nations General Assembly declares apartheid a crime against humanity.
>
> 1977—U.N. Security Council embargoes arms exports to South Africa.
>
> 1983—New constitution gives limited political rights to colored and Asian minorities.
>
> 1986—United States imposes broad economic sanctions.
>
> 1990—Mandela is released from prison. Legal end of segregation in public places.
>
> 1992–93—Apartheid is dismantled; black majority is enfranchised.
>
> 1994—First all-races election is held.

According to this time line, what actions were taken to end apartheid? List three.

_____

_____

_____

_____

_____

(continued)

DBQ 23: HUMAN RIGHTS

Document 5

Below is a simulated newspaper headline from June 1989 in Beijing.

> Chinese Army Crushes Pro-Democracy Protesters Assembled in Tiananmen Square

According to this newspaper headline, what human right abuses occurred at Tiananmen Square?

_____

_____

_____

_____

Document 6

This excerpt is adapted from a Human Rights Watch report on the Taliban.

> (New York, November 1, 1998)—An August massacre of civilians by Taliban troops in Mazar-i Sharif is one of the worst atrocities of Afghanistan's long civil war, Human Rights Watch said in a new report released today. . . . According to eyewitnesses quoted in the report, Taliban troops taking control of Mazar-i-Sharif sought out and executed members of the Hazara ethnic group, who are Sh'ia Muslims. The Taliban are believers in a strict version of Sunni Islam.
>
> "In a very brutal war, this is a particularly brutal episode," said Patricia Gossman, senior researcher of Human Rights Watch's Asia Division. "We are talking about the systematic execution of perhaps 2,000 civilians, in large part because of their ethnic and religious identity."

Source: Human Rights Watch, "Survivors Describe Taliban—Human Rights Watch urges U.N. Investigation of Massacre," http://hrw.org/english/docs/1998/11/01/afghan1424.htm, 1998 (adapted)

According to Human Rights Watch, what group's human rights were violated by the Taliban government in Afghanistan, and why?

_____

_____

(continued)

DBQ 23: HUMAN RIGHTS

Document 7

The following excerpt includes a description of the war in Afghanistan.

> In October 2001, the United States began bombing Taliban air defenses, airfields, and command centers. . . . In December, the Taliban were driven from power, but the fight to destroy al-Qaeda continued. Meanwhile, the United Nations worked with . . . Afghan groups to establish an interim government to replace the Taliban.

Source: Roger B. Bech, *World History: Patterns of Interaction,* McDougal Littell, 2002 (adapted)

What actions were taken against the Taliban, and by whom? _____

_____

_____

Document 8

This excerpt is adapted from the Statute of Amnesty International.

> **Vision and Mission**
>
> Amnesty International's vision is of a world in which every person enjoys all of the human rights enshrined in the Universal Declaration of Human Rights and other international human rights standards. . . .
>
> **Methods**
>
> . . . Amnesty International seeks to disclose human rights abuses accurately, quickly, and persistently. It systematically and impartially researches the facts of individual cases. . . . These findings are publicized, and members . . . mobilize public pressure on governments and others to stop the abuses.

What does Amnesty International do to stop human rights abuses?

_____

_____

_____

 PART B How have the human rights of three specific groups of people around the world been violated? What actions have been taken to stop each of these abuses? How effective have these actions been?

DBQ 23: TEACHER PAGE

Grading Key

Document 1

Millions of people were killed. Cambodians were forced to work long hours and to move from the city to the countryside. The Communists, or the Khmer Rouge, tried to completely change the country. This was a violation of people's rights to life, liberty, and security of person.

Document 2

Dith Pran hoped to tell the world about the Cambodian genocide by compiling a book, *Children of Cambodia's Killing Fields,* which told the story of survivors of the killing fields. He hoped to use the royalties from the book to make American students aware of what happened in Cambodia.

Document 3

The sign allowed only whites to use these public premises. This was a violation of the black South Africans' human rights to be free and equal in dignity and rights, regardless of race.

Document 4

Steps to end apartheid (students list three): U.N. General Assembly declared apartheid a crime against humanity; U.N. Security Council embargoed arms exports to South Africa; U.S. imposed economic sanctions; segregation in public places ended; black majority got right to vote.

Document 5

Protesters who were asking for democracy were forced to stop their protest; many were killed or arrested. This was a violation of the people's rights to freedom of opinion, peaceful assembly, and life.

Document 6

The Hazara people's rights were violated by the Taliban because of the Hazaras' ethnic and religious background.

(continued)

Document 7

The United States bombed Taliban installations and drove the Taliban out of power. The United Nations and Afghanis set up a new government that replaced the Taliban.

Document 8

Amnesty International tries to stop human rights violations by disclosing, researching, and publicizing specific violations. Members then mobilize public pressure to stop the abuses.

Additional Information Beyond the Documents

These documents provide students with only fragments of evidence. Essays should include relevant information beyond the documents—information that students have learned from their classroom study, outside reading and viewing, and other learning experiences. The following list suggests some of that information.

- United Nations Declaration of Human Rights
- Pol Pot and the Cambodian genocide
- Apartheid in South Africa and the work of Nelson Mandela and others to end it
- Taliban in Afghanistan
- Tiananmen Square and the Chinese government's handling of the protest
- Amnesty International